On the Goose

On the Goose

A Labrador Métis Woman Remembers

Josie Penny

DUNDURN
TORONTO

Editor: Jennifer McKnight
Design: Jennifer Scott
Printer: Webcom

Library and Archives Canada Cataloguing in Publication

Penny, Josie, author
          On the Goose : a Labrador Métis woman remembers / Josie Penny.

Issued in print and electronic formats.
ISBN 978-1-4597-1912-5 (pbk.).--ISBN 978-1-4597-1913-2 (pdf).--ISBN 978-1-4597-1914-9 (epub)

1. Penny, Josie. 2. Métis--Newfoundland and Labrador--Labrador--Residential schools. 3. Goose Bay (N.L.)--Biography. 1. Métis women--Newfoundland and Labrador--Labrador--Biography. I. Title.

FC109.1.P45A3 2014   971.82004'970092   C2013-906074-X   C2013-906075-8

1   2   3   4   5   18   17   16   15   14

We acknowledge the support of the **Canada Council for the Arts** and the **Ontario Arts Council** for our publishing program. We also acknowledge the financial support of the **Government of Canada** through the **Canada Book Fund** and **Livres Canada Books**, and the **Government of Ontario** through the **Ontario Book Publishing Tax Credit** and the **Ontario Media Development Corporation**.

Care has been taken to trace the ownership of copyright material used in this book. The author and the publisher welcome any information enabling them to rectify any references or credits in subsequent editions.

J. Kirk Howard, President

The publisher is not responsible for websites or their content unless they are owned by the publisher.

Printed and bound in Canada.

Visit us at
Dundurn.com | @dundurnpress | Facebook.com/dundurnpress | Pinterest.com/Dundurnpress

Dundurn	Gazelle Book Services Limited	Dundurn
3 Church Street, Suite 500	White Cross Mills	2250 Military Road
Toronto, Ontario, Canada	High Town, Lancaster, England	Tonawanda, NY
M5E 1M2	LA1 4XS	U.S.A. 14150

Contents

Acknowledgements

With much appreciation I am becoming increasingly aware of the work involved in putting a book together. The writing is just the beginning. First of all, I would like to thank Dundurn Press for accepting this second episode of my story. I would like to thank my daughter, Cathy Penny, who has just finished four years at McMaster University for her unwavering knowledge and help; Cathy never hesitated when I asked if she would edit my manuscript. Her speed with her laptop blew me away as she manipulated my messy tale into something that would make sense. Her skills made it possible to meet my deadline.

I would also like to extend a special thank you to my friend Elaine Boucher, who sat in my studio trying to correct my grammar without changing my words; putting *then* and *than* in the right places and encouraging me when I was in doubt. I'm also thankful to my siblings for helping me out in memory jams.

To our four children, Gregory, Darlene, Catherine, and Mark, I want to thank them so very much for allowing me to expose their childhood to the world. They came from strong, courageous stock and I am very proud of them. I want to acknowledge Mark and Cathy for, not only their computer and technical skills, but also their patience for my lack of them.

And Keith, what can I say? We were two very broken people trying to raise a family of four children without the life skills to even know how. He has been my biggest support, and he's pretty good at promoting my books as well. To all my employees, both as domestics, professional, and those not so professional, but were there for me — thank you all.

And finally, to all the people whose names are mentioned without permission, please forgive me. I don't even know where most of you are, but we could get in touch through Facebook or in person if you care to reach me. My life is an open book — literally.

Introduction

It was difficult coming up with a title for this book.

Several titles came to mind over the course of writing the next seventeen years of my journey. Goose Bay, Labrador, was a transient military base. Once the forces moved out, people who had lived in Goose Bay for a number of years then moved on to other parts of the world. Anyone who had lived there affectionately referred to it as *on the Goose*. Happy Valley came to be as a result of the civilians who helped build both the Canadian and Americas bases. When talking of *on the Goose*, it could refer to all areas of Happy Valley and Goose Bay.

When I arrived there in 1960 it was still a pioneer town without a lot of the amenities that one expects. With the help of my publisher Dundurn, in Toronto, we selected this title from several that I'd suggested.

The seventeen years I spent on the Goose was anything but tranquil, peaceful, or fulfilling. My work as an employee and an entrepreneur, my duties as a mother, and my dedication to my husband and friends pushed me, at times, beyond my ability to cope.

This story takes place in Happy Valley and Goose Bay, located in Central Labrador. Some names have been changed to protect relatives and friends who were entangled in my life.

At age eighteen, I met and married my husband Keith and gave birth to four beautiful children before the age of twenty-four.

In recent years I've heard Labrador being called "The Big Land" and for good reason: three areas the size of Newfoundland Island can fit within the boundaries of Labrador, which has a total population of approximately 28,000, primarily made up of Caucasian, Inuit (Eskimo), Innu (Indian), Metis, and European settlers. These settlers married aboriginals, resulting in the majority of Métis Labradorians today.

In 1961 when I moved to Happy Valley, there were 2,861 people. It doubled in 1966 to 4,415. After the amalgamation of Spruce Park and the Department of Transport housing areas in 1970, the population grew to approximately 7,000 people.

How did Happy Valley–Goose Bay get started? It's a long, drawn-out story, but the short of it is this: During the Second World War three countries — Great Britain, the United States, and Canada — had decided they needed airfield facilities as final stopover and re-fuelling sites before crossing to Europe, and to provide security to the Northern Hemisphere.

In May 1941, Captain Roosevelt and Dr. Forbes from the United States headed the expedition to find a suitable location for an airbase. After searching Hebron in Northern Labrador and Baffin Island they came to a place near North West River in Central Labrador, and chose the area around Lake Melville.

The Canadian Privy Council reported at the July 1941 meeting that the Minister of National Defence and its board construct a base on the Western coast. They had already been surveying the area as a possible site for their base. After much study it was decided that Goose Bay's sandy plateau, known as the bench, was the most suitable.

Goose Bay had a relatively clear, dry climate and was accessible by sea through the Hamilton Inlet into Terrington Basin. It was decided that all three countries work jointly to build the massive airfields, which later became Goose Bay International Airport. The airfields served three distinct military bases: the Royal Canadian Air Force, the United States

Air Force, and a small contingency of Royal Air Force as well. Goose Bay prided itself on having one of the largest runways for aircraft in the Western Hemisphere.

McNamara Construction offered to build the base or bases. It was a colossal job, to be sure. Shiploads of steel, wood, and all forms of building materials were off-loaded from ships in Terrington Basin, which had to be dredged to make it accessible for the ships to enter it, then transported to the newly chosen sites. Shacks were constructed for the workers, and so work began. Strong, proud individuals of all races and geographical locations left their homelands and headed for Goose Bay, Labrador, and a promise of a better life.

I would like to apologize for any inaccuracies in this story that other people may see or remember differently. My portrayal of Goose Bay in the sixties and seventies is true to my story as I saw it.

Enjoy!

Chapter 1

Happy Valley

On a warm, sunny day in July 1960, I was filled with excitement, anticipation, and apprehension as the old ship moved closer and closer to my new world. My boyfriend, Murray, had gotten me a job in Happy Valley, and as I clung to him, he tried to explain what it was like there. It's hard to describe the barrage of feelings as the old *Kyle* steamed her way into Goose Bay's only seaport, Terrington Basin. My friend, Linda Mullins, who'd moved back to Cartwright from Goose Bay several years earlier, had also tried to tell me what it was like.

"Where is Happy Valley?" I asked.

"It's difficult to explain unless you've been there at least once," she replied. "All I can say is that it's in Central Labrador and about a twelve-hour run on the steamer. It's a busy place with thousands of people, cars, trucks, and motorcycles." She went on to explain how it was built and how it operated. My curiosity piqued as Linda tried to explain to me how and why Goose Bay came to be. How it was rooted in the complexity of the military.

Goose Bay was made up of two bases belonging to the Canadian Armed Forces and the United States Air Force; each distinctly different and referred to locally as the Canadian side and the American side. Each had its own movie theatre and restaurants. Between the two they had every sporting facility found in any large city. The Americans had nightclubs with slot machines, buildings with racquetball, volleyball, basketball, and tennis courts, and a golf course. The Canadians had a hockey arena and curling club. It had a recreation centre which housed a swimming pool, a mezzanine floor for basketball, badminton, and ping-pong tables. They had their own store on base. There was also a club for each rank of military personnel, as well as a civilian club for all civilians working for them.

It was all beyond my capacity to understand. I didn't know what a club was. There'd never been one in my world.

"A swimming pool? My oh my! They must be some rich, hey Linda?" I marvelled.

Murray had been telling me for several years about the thousands of people, the many businesses, and the hundreds of vehicles that were in Goose Bay.

"I even own a motorcycle!" he said.

"You do?" I asked with wonder.

Murray Pardy had lived in Happy Valley since early childhood after being fostered by wonderful people such as Mr. and Mrs. Saunders. He'd been telling me for the past year that he wanted to take me back to Cartwright with him and that he would find me a job there. He'd promised to take me for a ride on his motorcycle and take me to the movie theatre. He told me he would take me out to dinner at Saunders' Restaurant. A restaurant? My mind was racing. *Only rich people went to those places.*

"Will the movie place have a stovepipe going up the centre of the room like at the one here?" I asked.

"No stovepipe. It's called a theatre, and the seats are arranged in a way so that you can see the whole screen." I was mystified as he tried to make me understand the seating arrangements of theatres.

While the old steamer chugged her way through the narrow channel and into Terrington Basin, I thought she would surely go aground and end up on the sandbar. But she made it through. I was told that years earlier the basin had been dredged out to allow the huge military ships to off-load the supplies used to build the Canadian and American bases during the Second World War.

It had been an exhilarating trip with Murray at my side all the way. I was overcome with emotions; excitement of course, nervousness for sure, apprehension, and some sadness at leaving my family so far behind. But with my young seventeen-year-old heart filled with love, we disembarked the *Kyle* and stood on a huge dock waiting for transport to Happy Valley.

"Whass dat black stuff on de road, Murray?" I asked.

"Pavement."

"Whass it dere for?"

"To make the road nice and smooth," he answered.

Beyond the paved road all I could see was sand everywhere; along the sides of the road, in the ditches, and in parking lots. Not a single rock was anywhere to be seen. The surrounding forest was a mixture primarily of spruce, but juniper, balsam, birch, and fir trees also make up the rich forests of Labrador. As we pulled off the dock, taking my first car ride ever, I noticed alder bushes lined the clear-cut roads. This was nothing like riding in the trucks on the rough roads in Cartwright. We were now driving up a winding incline and large buildings came into view. There in front of us stood the Canadian military base. Once we left the military base area and entered civilian territory, the pavement ended and we were riding on a sand and gravel road. We rumbled along for what seemed like forever to travel the seven or eight miles to Happy Valley.

We first ended up at Murray's adopted parents' house on Hamilton River Road. They were one of the first settlers of this town. After receiving a warm welcome and a refreshing cup of tea, Murray drove me to my new place of employment, Mr. and Mrs. Crawford's house on Grand Street. Barbara, as I was instructed to call her, was a pretty but fairly large woman with warm eyes and a welcoming smile. She introduced me to three blond children. Freckle-faced Bernie, the oldest, would have been an excellent character in a Huck Finn movie. Gordon was a handsome young boy, and Joan was the youngest, with dancing blue eyes.

Mrs. Crawford showed me to my room. I laid my suitcase down and checked out my new home. Although it was small, at least I had my own space, which pleased me greatly. *What now?* I thought. *What will I have to do here?* I wasn't overly concerned about having to do housework. I knew all about housework. I decided to be patient and wait it out. Besides, I was rather shy, and although I'd always been inquisitive when at home, I clammed up around strangers.

My primary job was to care for the children. I was only on the job a couple of weeks when I started to cook supper for the family. Barbara seemed to be tired when she came home from work. Shortly after that I was running the whole household. Mr. Crawford was working for the town as a heavy equipment operator, and when he came home from work he was all greasy and tired looking. I was shy around him as well, and didn't know what to say, so I said nothing.

One night after supper when I was released from duty, I got ready to go out with my boyfriend. I was so excited! I wore pink and black because I was told they were sexy. I applied my makeup with the greatest of care and brushed my long, wavy hair until it glistened under the overhead light. I was ready! Murray picked me up on his motorcycle and we took off. It was exhilarating, but I was a little scared as we sped along the sandy road. I clung to him with all my might. We ended up at Saunders' Restaurant, just down the road from where I lived. He ordered chips.

"Whass chips?" I asked Murray.

"They're just deep fried potatoes. You'll like 'em," he assured me. "Some people call them french fries."

"Why do you call 'em chips den?"

"You sure do ask a lotta questions," he answered.

They were delicious. When he said chips, I thought of wood chips. Mom used to collect them in her apron to start the fire. I cooked chips at Lockwood School, but we'd called them french fries. We'd never had enough oil to cook them at home. Mom cut up potatoes and fried them in our huge iron frying pan along with fatback pork and onions. She would do stewed potatoes, which I didn't like at all. I enjoyed it when she allowed us to bake them and smother them in butter. And now we were enjoying chips. We could also have them smothered with gravy. They were the best!

A few days later, as we approached Saunders' Restaurant, there was several teenagers hanging around outside the restaurant and talking about going to a movie. The theatre was just down the road on Grenfell Street. I couldn't believe my ears as they continued to talk about movies, Elvis Presley, or things I had only read about in magazines. Growing up in my tiny town of Cartwright I'd read many stories in true story magazines about movie theatres, dinner theatres, restaurants, and the outside world in general, but I never thought I could be a part of it. After all, weren't they just for rich people? I watched with interest and curiosity the carryings-on of all the teenagers who'd gathered around the grounds outside the restaurant. Marty, who seemed to be the leader, had a girlfriend, Joyce, who I thought was very beautiful and seemed to be the focal point of the group. There were several others to whom I had not yet been introduced. I felt isolated and apart from the group. Murray put his arm around my waist and I felt protected and loved for the moment.

He ordered me on his motorcycle and I obeyed. We sped to the theatre, walked up the wide wooden stairs and into the foyer, and purchased our tickets.

"Whass dat?" I asked as we stood in line watching a lady fill huge bags with a scoop.

"Popcorn," he simply answered.

We entered a very dark room with a huge screen displaying cowboys on horseback. I'd read lots of books about cowboys when I was little. I remembered longing to ride off into the sunset and be free. I *was* free, free for the first time ever, and I felt happy as we snuggled together in the darkness of the theatre. I don't remember what the movie was called or anything about it. I was in awe of the whole experience. I munched on the most delicious popcorn.

After returning to the restaurant and chumming with his buddies, we all left. I enjoyed a fun evening in the long Labrador twilight, joking and laughing, taking fibs and rude remarks from them.

"Where did you find her, in an igloo?" one of the guys barked.

"She's cute. Wanna share her?" another quipped.

I recoiled and tucked my tiny body behind Murray.

"I wanna go home," I stammered.

So, without hesitation, he drove me home to the Crawfords'. We kissed passionately and he told me not to pay any attention to the idiots and that they meant no harm. I clung to him as one would to a life raft.

"I wanna go back home, Murray. I don't like your friends. They scare me," I cried.

"Oh Josie, they really don't mean to hurt you."

"Gotta go in now," I mumbled. "Good night." I tiptoed into the house and into my bedroom. It felt so alien to me. My feelings were all mixed up. What was I doing here in this strange place where I knew no one, where I didn't have any family members whatsoever, where people were mean spirited? Suddenly I felt so alone. *It'll be alright*, I told myself. *I'll be alright.*

Chapter 2

Finding Family

I liked working for Barbara Crawford and I adored the children. I settled into my job and enjoyed the freedom she allowed me to run the household. She appreciated my cooking their meals each night. Then, after supper, I was allowed to get dressed up and go out.

Murray loved me. I knew that because he kept telling me so. I wasn't sure if I loved him as much. I did appreciate him, especially in getting me out of Cartwright and getting me a job. I liked his kisses. They were warm and passionate, which made me lose myself.

It was shortly after I arrived in Happy Valley that I saw a guy in Saunders' Restaurant — a really cute guy. I was sitting with a friend who was visiting from Cartwright. And we were eating chips ... again. He stopped by our table and was tugging on my friend's jacket and making some remark to her. I stared at him and kept staring at him, but he paid no attention to me whatsoever. I fell-head-over-heels in love the moment I set eyes on him!

I thought he was very handsome. He stood about five feet ten inches, slim, and had huge hands, sandy hair, and the bluest eyes I'd ever seen.

He was wearing a Hudson's Bay striped jacket. I assumed he knew I was new in town. Then Murray came through the door.

"Hi Keith," Murray mumbled, giving him an odd look as he sidled past Keith and made a motion for me to join him. I reluctantly got up and joined him. We left together on his motorcycle. As we sped down the road Murray didn't say much. We stopped at the river and sat in silence. I couldn't stop thinking of Keith. At least I knew his name now.

"Who is Keith?" I asked Murray.

"Das Keith Penny, and he's a loud-mouthed bum," he said to me in a tone I wasn't familiar with.

"He don't look like a bum. He looks good to me."

"Oh yah? Josie, you're *my* girl, and I *love* you so much," he crooned, nuzzling my neck.

"Is ya jealous Murray?" I asked. "Besides," I continued, "he didn't even pay any attention to me. He was too busy teasing Beulah."

Suddenly I felt uncomfortable. What was happening? Murray and I had been lovers for over two years! Each summer he'd come to Cartwright to be with me. I felt somewhat guilty because all I could think of was Keith, who, as I said, hadn't noticed me at all! Was it me he was trying to reach when he was teasing Beulah, but didn't quite know how?

Murray and I necked for a while on the grassy riverbank. Something had changed in me. I faked the emotions to keep the peace, but my mind was racing. I would have to wait for another chance meeting with Keith. There were several other guys in his group of friends that I thought were cute as well. Later I laid on my bed and thought of Marty Parsons. He seemed to be very popular in the group and was so handsome with the Elvis Presley hairdo. Was I boy crazy?

While doing my chores the next day I thought of Keith again. I wondered where he lived, where he worked. Did he have a car? How old was he? And on and on. Until then, I had never felt so intensely emotional about anyone in my life. I would have to wait another few hours and hopefully he would be at Saunders' again. It was the hangout for many young people. There were several tall, beautiful girls as well: Brooks, Madeline, Pauline, and Joyce. Joyce was Marty's girlfriend and very beautiful, with blond hair and blue eyes that jumped out at you from a flawless face. Compared to their tall statures, my short, four foot, eleven inch frame matched the feelings of my insides and the perception that I did not measure up to their beauty. It seemed the boys I liked already had girlfriends and the ones that wanted to date me were weird. This was too much! There were too many choices, too many boys interested in me, too much attention, and too many mixed emotions. I didn't have the wherewithal to handle them. My seventeen-year-old mind was thrown into chaos.

The following evening Murray took me farther down Hamilton River Road to his friend Abe Webber's house. It was a common occurrence for Abe to have parties that involved beer, a drink I had not yet tried. It was during this party I found out something that would change the dynamics of my life here: Abe was related to me through his brother Ken. Ken Webber was married to my father's sister, Winnie. A real aunt? I had family here after all! I was delighted.

"Will you take me to see her, Murray?" I begged as soon as we left the house.

"Okay, Josie, we'll go."

As we sped along the road, my mind was focusing on what I'd heard Mom and Dad say about them. I remembered little, except that they had visited Cartwright in the late fifties. I wished I had paid better attention. Suddenly I remembered a story. That wee Vivian, the youngest of Aunt Winnie's five children, had been accidently shot by her father, Ken. Some of their other children were grown and married.

We pulled into a driveway on Grand Street where a single, rundown bungalow perched on a sandy lot looked like it could use some repair. As I stepped inside and saw my Aunt Winnie I cried. She reminded me of Aunt Emma Winters from Muddy Bay; a two-family community just outside of Cartwright. I could see the resemblance to my dad. I felt akin to her immediately. She was a short, plump woman with warm brown eyes and wispy salt and pepper hair. Like my dad and Aunt Emma she also walked with a slight limp.

"Josie! My, my, my, you're all grown up," she said, giving me the warmest hug I'd had in a long time. I didn't want to let go of her for fear she'd disappear. "Well," she continued, "you didn't grow very tall, but you're a pretty little thing."

"Tank you," was all I could mumble.

Her children, Archie, Olive, Marina, and Vivian, were there. What a comforting feeling to know I had real family here and that I wasn't so alone anymore. I grew to love this woman very much. Like my father and my Aunt Emma she was a gentle soul, a kind and caring person.

I lay on my bed after work the next evening, taking a breather before getting ready to go out. I thought of this family of Curls. Where had they come from? In my altered state as a teenager I'd had no time to think of such things. While living at home with my mother I was always angry or hurt at the way she treated me. I had to work hard, I had to do everything *right*. I had to do as she said or get a *lacin'*. I had to look after all the little babies that seemed to come every year. Even though I loved all of them, I resented having to babysit them. As an adolescent I'd become a tomboy and choose whenever possible to be with my father or big brother. I'd had no time to think of family. What was a family anyway? I'd been sent away to a hospital at age four because my head was torn up by husky dogs. I was sent away to boarding school at age seven, because there were no schools on the Labrador coast. I was sent out to work at age eleven because my mom and dad needed help to feed the babies that kept coming every year, and as an adolescent I did hours and hours of babysitting for several Cartwright residents, and was sexually molested by a couple of them. At age fifteen I moved out of the family home and worked for the Mission that I'd attended as a little girl, and now, at age seventeen, I moved away from my hometown forever. What would I know about home or a family setting? Would I ever see them again? Tears soaked into my pillow. Yes, I had freedom, but freedom from what? And at what price?

Chapter 3

Dating Games

Black and pink — those were the colours I was told were sexy. I craved love and attention. I wanted to be sexy, so I bought myself sexy new clothes. I'd get dressed up in my black skirt with lots of crinoline underneath, pull on my sexy pink top, brush my long wavy hair, and head to Saunders'.

I entered the restaurant and a group of girls were sitting at a table. They didn't invite me to join them, and it looked like they were talking about me as my tiny frame meandered to a table and slid into a booth. I jutted my chin out and paid no attention. I was the new girl in town and a threat to them. *They're just afraid I'll take their boyfriends away from them,* I thought. There had been several guys milling around outside and whistled as I passed them. I loved those cat calls. I knew I looked sexy, and to me that was all that mattered.

As I was sitting at a table all alone, a guy named Tom sauntered in. He came directly toward me and sat down.

"Josie, is it?" he asked with interest.

"Yah. How did you know my name?"

"You're the new girl in town," he said. "Would you like to go for a car ride?"

I'd noticed a few fellows in nice cars milling around Saunders' but thought they were much too good to talk to me. I thought they must be rich to own such beautiful cars.

"Yes, I'd like that," I said. So we left. I plastered myself in this huge car and tufted my crinoline just so as we took off down the road, spewing up a thick cloud of smoke, dust, and sand behind us. I was thrilled! I hadn't been in many cars before. After all, I hadn't even seen one until I came here! I felt exhilarated and happy. *This is the life,* I thought.

"Where are you from, Josie?" Tom asked.

"Cartwright. I came on the *Kyle* last week. I work for the post mistress," I said, trying to sound grown up.

"That's interesting. Do you like working there? How do you like Happy Valley?"

As the small talk continued, I was thinking of where I was: in a huge car with a nice-looking, clean-cut man and heading for god knows where. We ended up on a hilltop in the woods. Suddenly, I felt scared. Was he going to rape me? My mind went back to that terrible time in the woodshed at Lockwood Boarding School. I'd been pinned down by several boys and gang raped. I was only nine at the time.

We sat and talked for a long time. I began to relax a little and thought that if he was going to rape me, he would have by now. We started necking. I didn't have the tools to fight off his demands. This world was strange and new to me and there was so much I didn't understand. Up to that point in my life I hadn't heard about being easy or cheap, or about being called a slut or whore. What were they? I certainly didn't know that guys put notches in their belts every time they had sex with a girl! I didn't know anything! Did I feel anything? Guilt? Shame? I'd lost my sense of self as a very young child and was conditioned to obey, to submit, and to do as I was told. I was powerless to resist. I just couldn't say *no*.

I didn't go out with him again. He never called. Did he win a bet in getting a date with the new girl in town? Did he win the bragging rights? I felt used and abused. I felt cheap. *Where's Murray?* I wondered. *Is he mad at me?* I needed his love — I needed something familiar, someone I could trust to care for me. *I'll call him in the morning,* I thought as I, once again, cried myself to sleep.

The next morning was bright and sunny. I felt invigorated and threw myself into getting the kids ready for another day and cleaning up the house. I liked it here with the Crawfords; it was an easy job. George was always working and came home tired. Barbara came home exhausted as well. After cleaning up the dinner dishes and tidying the living room, I called Murray.

"Where were you last night?" he asked right off the bat.

"I went for a ride with a guy."

"Who? And why?" he asked sadly.

I wouldn't tell him who, or why. It didn't seem to matter. I was getting tired of answering his questions. I just wanted to have a good time and experience new things. "It was just a stupid mistake!" I yelled. "I got caught up in the car thing. It's no big deal." The fight was on.

"I'll pick you up at seven o'clock tonight then, okay?" he asked.

"Alright," I replied, too exasperated to continue.

As Murray drove up, I hopped on his motorcycle and we took off to the riverbank. We embraced, but something had changed. It wasn't the same warm hug I was used to.

"Why did you cheat on me, Josie? You know I love you and it hurts me so much," he said. "I realize this is all new to you, and how you must feel. But you have to learn that it's not right to do what you're doin'. People will talk."

"I know, Murray, and I'm sorry," was all I could say. I went silent, my mind was racing. "People will talk," he'd said. Was I the talk of the town? Was I bad? Were people calling me that terrible word I hated so much? Was I a slut? I couldn't think about it. However, I *had* to think about it. I needed to decide whether I wanted to stay with Murray or break up. This was a strange new life with many exciting things to do and lots of places to go. I'd become overwhelmed and confused as to what to do next. I felt guilty at the thought of breaking up with him. After all, Murray and I had been dating for several years at this point. He had always been there for me. But more importantly, he'd gotten me here! I began to wonder if I'd ever really loved him. Yes, he had come to Cartwright every summer and we were inseparable during those times, but during the winter I would date whomever I pleased, and answered to no one. I lavished the attention I'd gotten from the GI's. I was captivated with their tales of faraway lands. I believed the nice things they whispered in my ear as we lay on the floor in the powerhouse in Cartwright. There were a few that I dated on a regular basis, but when I'd get a letter from Murray, I'd feel guilty.

"I'll let you know when I make up my mind, Murray," was all I could say.

A few days later I had another date. Jack picked me up in his car and we raced up the road toward the base. He took me to the Canadian military base and we entered the big theatre. I don't recall the movie, just the experience of sitting in this theatre, with the huge masks hanging on the wall on each side of the screen. It was a far cry from the little school house in Cartwright, with the stovepipe in the centre of the room obstructing my vision. Being in a real movie theatre made me feel important. Afterward we went to the airport snack bar next door for chips, or was it french fries? Whatever they were, I couldn't get enough of them. This was exciting! It was much bigger than Saunders' Restaurant in Happy Valley. Later, we went driving around town and ended up on Lover's Lane. That's what I'd heard it called by several people in town. I didn't want to end up on Lover's Lane. I wanted to go home. I was almost raped that night. Again. What was wrong with me? I escaped and walked all the way home to the Crawfords'.

As I lay on my bed with tears running onto my pillow I thought of home. Did they miss me? Did my dad miss my help getting the water and wood? Did he miss having me to go birdin' with him, or go jigging for codfish out in the run? I missed the lifestyle, the sea. I missed being able to take Dad's punt for a row, or go with him for a ride to Earl Island or Muddy Bay. Once while jigging for cod off Earl Island I accidently hooked the jigger into my thigh. Because it went in past the barb, Dad had to cut it free with his pocket knife. I still have that scar today. I'd learned to operate the little boat pretty good by the time I'd left home.

Every year Mom would find another baby somewhere. I guess it was just easier to say they were found then have to explain the cycle of life.

By this time though, I'd learned that they were *born* and not *found* somewhere; under a rock or in the land wash or in the bush. Wee sister Dora was the first of our family to be born in Cartwright. I was sad when she was stricken with tuberculosis and had to be sent away to St. Anthony Hospital in Newfoundland. She was gone for nine months. We'd lost another brother; wee Tony died a few years later. He was the fourth baby my mother had lost through illness. However, she raised ten of us to adulthood and primarily on her own after Dad died suddenly in 1967.

I loved all of my siblings and I missed them terribly. Through no choice of my own I'd always had to work or babysit for several people and go to school, therefore I'd had little time to get to know them very well. Would I ever get to know them? Baby brother Phillip was so cute. Mom loved him very much and spoiled him to no end. Baby sister Linda was adorable also.

Suddenly my body was flushed with guilt. I'd abandoned my family forever! There were no phones in Cartwright yet. I couldn't even talk to them. So, there I was, sad and lonely and wondering if anyone would love me — really love me and not just want to have sex with me! Why did all the boys want to have sex? I didn't understand. I was able to say no to Jack and escaped yet another possible rape. I felt terribly alone.

A few days later I heard there was going to be a party, and I was invited to go. I can't recall who invited me, or how I ended up there. Why would they invite me? It was held at a big fancy house down on Hamilton River Road. I entered the room and almost ran back out when I saw all the people. Then I spotted Keith. He was sitting, cracking jokes, and laughing with his buddies. I don't know if he noticed me or not. The party went as well as parties go, but I was feeling shy and inferior. I tried to melt into the walls. Everyone started playing a game called Post Office. It's where you spin the bottle and whoever it's pointing to when it stops gets to take a member of the opposite sex into a room for a few minutes. Several people were in that room for longer than a few minutes. I wondered what they were doing in there. It was my turn. Round and round went the bottle, and eventually it stopped. It was pointing straight at Keith. I thought I was going to faint right then and there!

As we entered the room we looked awkwardly at each other. He embraced me gently and kissed me on the mouth ever so lightly. His lips were silky soft. I trembled as a second kiss became more passionate.

"Will you meet me at the restaurant tomorrow night?" he whispered in my ear.

"Yes," I crooned, rather breathless.

I walked back into the party in awe. My whole body was trembling. I thought I was going to faint! What was it about him that excited me so?

I went through the motions of cleaning the house the next day, feeding the children, making the beds, and all the other chores that needed to be done in the run of a day. I thought of the upcoming evening. What would I wear? My pathetic wardrobe offered few sexy garments. Some of the clothes I had brought with me were from the rag-bag my mother had brought from the Mission as payment for her sewing. *I'm gonna go shopping when I get paid, that's for sure,* I thought as I polished off the living room furniture. In the meantime I'd have to dig out my pink blouse and black slacks again.

Keith picked me up in the tiniest car I'd ever seen. Not that I'd seen much of any type of car up to that point. It was a yellow Prince. As we sped down the road with a cloud of sand dust billowing up behind us, I felt happy. We were simply driving around town, not saying much.

Suddenly the car filled with smoke. Something was on fire! We had to escape quickly for fear of it exploding. Keith wasn't sure what was wrong, so we hadn't any choice but to walk back to the restaurant and endure the wisecracks, giggles, and smirks from his buddies.

"Pretty hot stuff there, eh Keith?" someone snickered.

"Yeah, if she's that hot maybe I ought to try her myself," one of the other guys piped up.

"Boy oh boy, you got a hot chick this time, eh buddy?"

I felt embarrassed and ashamed. I felt like crawling into a hole, but I knew nothing had happened, so I endured the teasing. We walked into Saunders' and ordered a plate of chips with gravy, then we walked to the theatre to see a movie. I wanted to melt into my seat because those brainless guys had made me feel cheap. Maybe I was cheap, maybe I did have a reputation of being easy, and maybe I did deserve the gossip. All that really mattered was that I was with Keith; I was in love. Afterward he walked me home holding my hand, which practically disappeared in his large one. We tucked our trembling bodies tightly against the clapboard siding and I placed my hand on his face as we kissed passionately.

"Would you like to come inside?" I asked him.

"Oh no, that wouldn't be right," he replied.

"The Crawfords won't mind," I crooned, as our temperatures rose to dangerous levels. "They don't mind what I do. I'm not their child. I'm free to do what I want after work."

Mrs. Crawford was so happy with my work that we never discussed house rules, and even if we had, I really didn't care at that point. I wanted to feel loved. I needed it. I craved it. And I was going to get it!

We tiptoed into the house and into my bedroom, which, thankfully, was the first room, just across the kitchen, and eased ourselves onto the bed. I would like to say that I was a good girl, that he would be the first and that I was a virgin, but the opposite was true. I certainly didn't know that Keith was inexperienced at that point, but sensed something very special about him. I just wanted him so. I had driven him to the point of no return and we awkwardly, but tenderly made love that night.

Chapter 4

Falling in Love

I fell in love with Keith Penny from the very first time I met him. I have heard many times since those tender years that love at first sight sometimes does indeed happen.

At the risk of being teased by his buddies, we met almost every night at Saunders' Restaurant. I didn't know at the time that Keith had dated several of the local girls, most of whom were tall and beautiful. Once I found out I kept thinking, *why he would want to have anything to do with such a little person as me?* We continued to date every night through August and September. We became a couple and I didn't care what any of the other so-called pals were saying or what any of the girls were talking about. I was very much in love!

We dated through the fall of 1960. I did my work during the day and at night, if I wasn't going out with him, I would walk up the road around the corner to his house and wait for a glimpse of him through his window. I'd watch him comb his hair and put his Hudson's Bay striped jacket on and head for the door. I wondered where he was going. However, I wasn't emotionally strong enough to come out of the bushes and face him. I didn't tell him this until years later. We spent a lot of time at the movies, and jostling with his buddies. We went to house parties and we made love in the twilight.

In this small town of Happy Valley, it was impossible to hide anything from anybody. Because there was only one hangout, it didn't take long for Murray to find out. He knew what was happening and I knew he knew, but I was smitten with Keith. As far as I was concerned Murray and I were through. But, how would I tell him? How was I going to just drop him now? Well I didn't tell him. I just couldn't! I couldn't face the pain I knew would be on his face. So I just kept going out with Keith.

I was walking to the restaurant a few days later when Murray came by on his motorcycle.

"What's goin' on Josie?" he asked.

"I want to break up, Murray. I have a new boyfriend now."

"Ya, I heard about your new boyfriend," he mumbled. "Then we're through?"

I shuffled the sand with my foot, not knowing where to look or what to say. Again, guilt engulfed me as I tried to soften the reality of what was happening. My mind was racing. *Didn't I deserve to be with whomever I wanted to be with? Hadn't I earned the freedom I'd longed for for so long?* We were at a loss for words. There was no argument, no confrontation, just the saddest look in his eyes I'd ever seen.

"I love Keith," I finally told Murray.

He drove silently away.

Keith and I had a short but very active courtship. He took me to lots of movies and afterward we would go "parkin."

Keith and I started going to church together. We were even talked into selling church calendars door to door! This pleased his parents greatly, and gave them confidence that we were on the right track. Even though I never felt accepted by them, they did their best to make me feel all right; to make me feel accepted. But, unfortunately for me, I never felt it. I felt inferior and that was that.

I was not prepared for what happened next. When I missed my monthly period, I had no idea why. I knew nothing about the cycle of life other than what my friend Linda Mullins had told me in Cartwright several years earlier. She didn't go so far as to say what would happen if I became pregnant. So, when I missed two periods, I became very concerned. What would I do? Where would I go if I lost my job? Would Keith leave me? So many questions. I had no one to answer them, and no one to confide in. I hadn't even a single friend yet. So, when I missed the third month, I had to tell Mrs. Crawford.

"It sounds like you might be pregnant," she said.

"Pregnant?" It took a few seconds for that word to register in my brain. Pregnant?

"You're going to have a baby, Josie. You had better go to the clinic and check it out."

I couldn't be pregnant! I'd just met Keith. I'd only been here a few months. I was just starting my new life in this place.

Keith knew even less than me about such basic things as the monthly cycle or fertility. He had never even heard the word "pregnant" before. When I missed the fourth month I had no choice but to tell him. I knew he was picking me up for the Christmas party at the town hall that night, and I would tell him then. He picked me up in his car and I crawled inside and slammed the door. I was shaking from fear of what he would say or do. But something told me that I had to press on.

"I think I'm pregnant, Keith," I blurted.

"What! What do you mean pregnant? Whass dat?"

"I haven't had a period for almost four months and I think I'm gonna have a baby."

He went silent, trying to absorb what I'd just told him. Trying to understand what it all meant.

"'Tis not mine then, dat's for damn sure. You've been out with dozens of fellers and it could be anybody's!" he screamed.

"No, Keith! I haven't been with a single person since I met you. You were the only one since our very first date."

"Did you go to the nurse yet? How can you be sure?"

"I'm goin' tomorrow," I murmured through my tears.

What will I do if he leaves me? I thought. *I'll lose my job. I'll have no place to live, no one to turn to.* I was terrified, alone, and having those terrible feelings of abandonment and rejection again. Then I thought of Aunt Winnie. She wouldn't turn me away, would she? But I didn't want to live with her. She had enough to worry about with a whole bunch of youngsters and a husband, who, in my opinion, drank too much. They didn't look like they were very well off, either.

My mind circled back to the present. *What have I got myself into now?* I thought. *Where did my plans of freedom and a carefree life in this big town go?* Suddenly my dreams of fun, of freedom, of everlasting happiness with the person I loved were blown to smithereens. I thought of what Mom might say. I was glad I wasn't home to hear her yelling and screaming, her cursing and swearing, her degrading comments. *I can deal with this,* I thought. *I have to!*

After that initial fight Keith seemed to change. He became kinder and somewhat compassionate toward me. There was no mention of the baby and we continued to spend time together for the rest of the fall and into the winter. I was so distraught that I don't remember anything about my first Christmas away from home. Where were all my dreams? Where was my tall, dark, and handsome man who would take care of me forever?

I did a lot of babysitting after work because I was unable to say no to people. One night while we were babysitting for the Seawards I was browsing through the Simpsons-Sears catalogue. We came upon the wedding dresses. Keith pointed to the most expensive one there, $29.95, and asked, somewhat fearfully, "Do you think you could still fit into one of those?"

I didn't know what to say. Was he proposing? I simply said, "I don't know. I guess I could order one and see if it fits."

I went home full of hope. I did love him very much. The feeling of abandonment lifted to a controllable level, and I fell asleep thinking for the first time in weeks of the tiny baby growing inside of me.

Chapter 5

The Penny Family

Mark Penny, Keith's father, was a descendent of an English family. He was offered a job in Buffalo, New York, and moved to Toronto. He commuted daily from Toronto to Buffalo for several years. In 1919, Mr. Penny received a letter from Bain Johnson & Company in Battle Harbour, Labrador, requesting him to come to Labrador to run its fishing operations. Dr. Grenfell saw Mark Penny as an enterprising young man and thought it would be smart to get him on his team. He approached Mark and offered to send him, all expenses paid, to Bishop Feild College in St. John's for teachers' training. After a few years of college, Mark returned to Labrador. As a young man he was a teacher, catechist, and lay reader in the Church of England. This he did for the rest of his working days. As a result, he became a prominent citizen of Labrador and was respected in every community he visited. Unfortunately for the Penny family, he received little pay for his efforts. He only earned seven hundred dollars a year, which was surely not enough to support a large family.

Mark married a widow with two small children and moved with them to Cartwright to teach school. He also travelled long distances on the Labrador coast by dog team during the winter months and by small boat during the summer months. With very little pay he travelled to all the communities along the coast, baptizing babies, performing marriages, praying for the sick and dying, and burying the dead. Payment could be a pair of moccasins, a pipe, hand-knit socks and mittens, a tool of some kind — anything other than money. With barely enough to feed his ever-growing family he did the best he could under extremely primitive conditions. He often left his wife and small children to fend for themselves in order to take care of the spiritually starved people and to teach as an itinerant teacher. This took its toll on the whole family. Hardships and hunger were the results. Mr. and Mrs. Penny raised eight children.

Keith Loomis Penny was born August 15, 1940, in Port Hope Simpson, Labrador. He was the youngest of nine to Mark and Elsie. Mr. Penny was fifty-six years old and Elsie was forty-seven when this healthy, blond-haired bundle of joy graced the Penny home. I would assume at those late years they did not plan to have a newborn. He was an inquisitive, mischievous child, and, to poor little Keith's consternation, as an adolescent he was handed around to several of his siblings, who by now were married with families of their own. He was left to do pretty much as he pleased. Keith told me one story of when he was only nine. His parents sent him on the *Kyle* with his brother George from Battle Harbour to Twillingate. He roamed all around the ship alone. The ship was dirty and by the time he reached Battle Harbour he was black from head to toe from coal dust. No one seemed to care where he went. He grew up without a sense of place, a sense of home, or a sense of belonging. It took its toll on the high-spirited, sensitive, soft-hearted person who grew into a fearful, insecure man with an oversized ego.

Keith didn't have the courage to tell his father about my pregnancy, so I had to tell him myself, which was traumatizing for me. He then approached Keith.

"What are you going to do about the young girl down the street?"

"I dunno. What about her?" Keith asked his father.

"She's going to have a baby, so you'll have to marry that girl. That's all there is to it!"

During the winter of 1961, my pregnancy was starting to show, and Keith and I were now disconnected from the few friends he'd been associated with for the past several years. I was pleased that he was so attentive, and that we spent a lot of time together, but I felt very uncertain about the future. A little later Keith and I became involved in community affairs. We sold church calendars door to door, and as a result of all of that we gained some semblance of respect from his family and Reverend Payne. We continued to participate in church activities with Keith's parents until a week after we got married. Then he stopped all activity with the church and I followed. It seemed as though Keith was just going to church to please his father.

In early May, I wrote to my mother telling her I was going to have a baby, and that my boyfriend Keith Penny was going to marry me. We hadn't yet set a date.

I waited anxiously for my dress to arrive. Finally it came in the mail and Mrs. Crawford brought it home. I ripped the package open and pulled it out. It was beautiful! The bottom had four tiers of wide lace and it had a lace-tiered bodice. With fear, I carefully let it drop over my shoulders and embrace my body. As I tried desperately to close the buttons, I couldn't! It was too small. In despair I pulled it off and checked the seams to see if they could be let out. I knew of a distant relative named Gladys who was an excellent seamstress. I decided I would ask her what she could do to make it fit. Shyly, with much misgiving, I knocked on her door and tried to explain my problem to her. We examined the dress and she figured out what she could do. In a few days she called me to try in on. With fear and trepidation I tried it on once again. It fit! I decided right then that the wedding would have to be soon.

So, I mailed another letter off to my mother to tell her we were getting married June 30, and asked if Sal could please come to be one of my bridesmaids. My sister Sarah, whom we always called Sal, arrived on the *Kyle* along with a letter from my mom. I'd never seen her handwriting before. With her grade three education, I cherished her scribbles, giving me blessings and wishing me happiness. Shortly afterward Sal arrived on the *Kyle*. I was so happy to see my sister! She was a year younger than me. We laughed and cried as we embraced. Having Sal with me was very gratifying. I felt less alone, and it was one of very few of my wedding plans I took part in. I recall very little of the days leading up to my wedding day. My soon-to-be sisters-in-law, Margaret and Dorcass, took charge from there. They bought material to make tiny head pieces from a gauze material. I don't remember how I got my veil. I don't recall anything about invitations, bridesmaids' dresses, or a reception. I don't remember any decisions in what the men would wear, or even who they were! I knew nothing of a charge for the wedding ceremony, or if money would be needed for the reception afterward. I don't recall paying anything for anything.

One thing I do remember is that there wasn't a flower shop in Happy Valley at that time, so I took the initiative and ordered a dozen fresh red roses from Montreal. They were the first fresh roses I'd ever seen. They were exquisite! I stared at them and wept. Would they last for one day until the wedding, or would they wilt, kind of like my spirit of uncertainty? What had I gotten myself into? Is this what I wanted? I then felt my baby kick inside me, which jolted me back to reality. *Yes, Josie, you need security for your baby; you need to make things right by it.*

Keith had stopped carousing with his buddies and had been supporting me throughout my pregnancy. The question kept nagging at me: Did he really love me, or was he marrying me because his father ordered him to? Only time would tell.

Chapter 6

My Wedding Day

I woke up on my wedding day, June 30, 1961, and like a robot I went through the motions of preparing for my wedding. We were getting married in the Anglican Church. Reverend Payne had been assisting us in marriage preparedness classes for a couple of weeks prior to our wedding. I can't recall any of what the Reverend told us. My baby was very active inside me and occupied most of my thoughts.

I was extremely grateful for Sal, who would be the only member of my family to attend. I can't recall if my Aunt Winnie attended or not, though I'd grown to love her, but she probably did come. After I finally got my dress to fit my ever-enlarging body, collected my white gloves and shoes, and picked up my flowers from the airport, I returned to Margaret's to get dressed. I was so grateful my seamstress had done such a wonderful job on my wedding dress that my pregnancy didn't show much at all. For whatever reason, I hadn't gotten very big. Aside from my baby bump, I'd actually lost a lot of body weight while I was pregnant.

I knew very little about makeup, or how to apply it. I plastered on blue eye shadow, mascara, and lipstick. There wasn't a hairdresser in the area that I knew of yet, and my shoulder-length wavy hair did not want to cooperate. I didn't like my bangs, so I took the scissors and trimmed them off. Immediately I was sorry because I cut them much too short, which made me look rather saucy.

Margaret, Dorcass, and Sal were in the next room getting ready as well. They had pretty, pale pink mid-calf dresses and short gauze head pieces fastened to their heads, attached with a floret. They wore white gloves and carried tiny flower bouquets Dorcass had made. We were ready! Off we went to the church. The next thing I recall was the Reverend telling us:

"You are now man and wife. You may kiss the bride."

Was I dreaming or was this real? Is it possible to be so out of touch with reality as to not know what you're doing? I was a good bride and played the part well. *I'm married,* I kept telling myself. *I'm married.*

We then made our way to Keith's brother's house. It was there that Bruce and Dorcass had prepared our wedding reception. They lived in a modest but nicely decorated home on Markland Road in Happy Valley, not far from the church. Although there were few photos and well wishes, I felt a lot of gratitude for our reception. I didn't or hadn't taken part in any of the preparations; my in-laws did a nice job of trying to make it look somewhat like a wedding reception. Nice white tablecloths draped a large table with a beautiful vase of artificial flowers accompanying our three-tiered wedding cake. Thanks to Dorcass's artistic and creative abilities she had done a beautiful job. I was very pleased with it. There were several bowls of salads, a few plates of cold cuts, and a pot of rabbit stew. Smack in the middle of the table was a tower of white baker's bread. Reverend Payne even came to celebrate with us, as he was a personal friend of Keith's parents. I recall posing for a few flashing cameras. We did get a few pictures that I now cherish. It was not a wedding feast that will go down in the record books, but I felt we did the right thing under the circumstances. We were now married. We did what was expected of us, plain and simple.

I have no idea how much anything cost. Keith had sixty-five cents in the bank when we got married and had to borrow five dollars from his brother Graham to pay the minister. I hadn't any money because I had spent it on the seamstress to let the seams out of my dress and to pay for my roses.

After the reception we went to Keith's parents' house just around the corner from our reception location. We were to spend our wedding night in Keith's bedroom. I didn't even know what his bedroom looked like because out of respect for his parents we never went there. Mr. Penny, being a lay reader, a catechist, and an active member of the church, had to be respected at all cost.

Mr. Penny was like a god to me, but I felt no connection with Keith's mom. They were so old! Mr. Penny had snow white hair, and even though I sensed he was a kind and caring man, I was still afraid of him. To think I had to go to *their* home on our wedding night was terrifying! I was shaking in my new shoes and wedding gown as we entered his bedroom. Where was I going? What was I doing here? What was happening to me? I was like a rag doll at the end of a little girl's hand, being dragged into nothingness. Did I know what I was doing? Did I really want this? However, here I was. I will never forget what unfolded in front of me as we opened Keith's bedroom door.

The house itself was still under construction, so there was no paint on the walls and there weren't any curtains to the window yet. The floor was plywood. There was a single bed up against the wall, on the right side of the room. I almost tripped over this god-awful contraption on the floor! I didn't know what it was! It had a bunch of different length glass tubes sticking up from it, with tangled wires everywhere. It was scary looking. We sat on the bed for a moment and I must have been in some kind of trance or something, as I kept staring at it. Finally I asked Keith.

"Whass that ting on de floor?"

"That's my radio," he replied. "I'm fixin' it."

"Where's de case?"

"I took the case off cause it needs a couple new tubes."

Well, that explained what it was. He didn't even have a nightstand to put it on. We had nothing else to do but to go to bed. As we undressed, rather shyly, I draped my wedding dress over an old chair. I didn't know what to think. Did I even think at all? I was numb. We got into bed and embraced without saying a word. I was fearful of the future, but didn't know what to do about it. We just needed to get through this night.

"Do ya love me?" I asked him, as he fumbled around my big belly.

"Yeh," he mumbled.

I don't know if Keith loved me or not. He never told me. He couldn't utter those three little words, but I did love him and showed him in every way possible. Our wedding night was spent with the two of us awkwardly trying to make love in a squeaky single bed with an old, battered, case-less radio crackling on the floor, with its dusty tubes sticking up like tiny beacons in a lighthouse. With his parents in the next room, and my baby kicking inside me!

Chapter 7

Our First Home

In the week that followed our wedding night, I was worried and scared of what was going to happen to me. Here I was, a new bride, soon to be a new mother, crammed in with my in-laws in a tiny bedroom without any space to call my own, and without any support. All I was getting from Mrs. Penny was advice on how to live my life. She talked down to me and made me feel very insecure. I figured things would change when she saw how well I could keep a house. After all, I'd been doing it since I was eleven years old.

I really didn't know what Keith was up to in the first weeks following our wedding, but I would soon find out. Things happened so rapidly that it's hard to get the details straight. I was not happy living with his parents. During this time Keith worked with a man on the military base whose name was Carl. One day Carl heard that Keith had recently married and asked Keith if he would be interested in buying his house. He was having trouble selling it.

"I have no money to buy your house," Keith said.

"I don't need the money right away. If I can sell it I'd move to the United States. I don't trust anybody to pay me the required price," he said. "And no one around here has enough money to pay for it. You seem like a nice, solid young man, Keith. How would you like to buy my house?"

"How much you want for it?" Keith asked.

"I want $1,800 and you could pay for the house on the instalment plan."

At that stage of my life and during that time in Labrador, wives were treated like children, and I was no exception. I didn't have a voice and anything Keith decided to do would have to be all right. I just accepted it as so! He came home from work one day and shocked me into reality.

"I bought a house today," he said.

"Whaa? A house? Where?"

"On Grand Street, just down around the corner from here."

"Oh Keith, I'm so happy! When can we move in?"

"Right away, because the owner is leaving tomorrow for the United States."

A deal was reached. We would be the proud owners of our own little house — wow!

It was decided that we would pay him a certain amount per month. It would come with all the furniture, a generator for electricity, and Keith's brother Graham gave us a yellow 1957 Ford pick-up truck. We were overwhelmed with gratitude! We moved into our little house on Grand Street just one week after we were married. I was elated. Our very own little house! I was so happy, and I couldn't believe my luck; especially when I realized we were moving next door to my Aunt Winnie! I felt a little more secure, and that I was going to be alright. I might not feel so alone anymore.

In my own home, I could care for my baby my way, without my mother-in-law peeking over my shoulder. I could now cook my own meals, and be free from criticism. I wouldn't have to worry about Keith's parents following my every move and making me feel inadequate.

The house was sixteen by twenty-two feet, with three rooms: a bedroom, a tiny kitchen, and a living room. There was no bathroom, no running water, and no furnace. There was just a small wood and oil stove that didn't work well. There wasn't a water and sewer system on

Grand Street yet. We did have electricity, but we didn't have appliances. Nevertheless, I was pleased that we had our own space. There were a few sticks of furniture in the house: a chesterfield, a chair, and a coffee table. There was a bed in the bedroom and a chrome kitchen set with four chairs. I couldn't help but think of my tiny playhouse on the hillside near the dormitory at Lockwood Boarding School. For whatever reason, I kept comparing everything to my childhood experiences.

I found a few lace doilies in a tiny closet in the house when we moved in. Things had happened so fast! Someone donated a crib. A few days later I was surprised once again when my sisters-in-law Dorcass and Margaret held a baby shower for me. I was in tears. No one had ever done so many wonderful things for me before. At the tender age of eighteen, I would have my very own baby, very own home, my very own husband who had a job and came home every day after work. And, I was extremely grateful for Aunt Winnie living next door. What more could a young bride ask for?

As soon as we settled into the house I set about preparing the baby's room and thinking about what my baby would look like. Would it be a boy or girl? Would it be healthy? Would Keith know what to do? How to care for it? How to love? I took each tiny garment and caressed it gently, trying to visualize my baby in it. I separated the colours and arranged them in the crib. One would think that after all I'd been through, living with my family back home in Cartwright and having to care for six of my siblings at such a young age, that I would want to run from another such responsibility. But maybe it had the opposite effect on me. I longed for my baby to come. I was excited to be a new mother. I couldn't wait!

In the meantime, Keith was trying to adjust to married life. When he came home each day after work, he seemed to be uncomfortable. I often wondered many times since then what he would have done if we hadn't *had* to get married. Maybe I'll never know for sure.

Chapter 8

First Born

Happy Valley was, to some degree, still a pioneer town when I arrived. The medical treatment facilities and conditions were fairly primitive in Happy Valley in 1961. There wasn't a hospital yet, just a small clinic on Hamilton River Road. It was headed by a German nurse named Susan. Prior to Susan arriving, babies were born by midwives or by somebody who had the courage, strength, and knowledge of how to do such things.

We were just nicely getting settled in our new home, when a few days later I woke up with cramps. I don't know why I didn't think it could be the baby wanting to make its way into the world, but I didn't. I never knew that hard cramps that lasted the whole night might be the birth of our baby. I didn't wake Keith up, and suffered in silence all night long, thinking I'd eaten something.

Keith got up and prepared for work. I had to grit my teeth as the pain ripped through my body. Finally, as he was going out the door I said, "Keith, I have hard cramps in my belly. It could be something I ate!"

He stopped for just a few seconds before leaving and mumbled, "Maybe you should call Margaret."

Margaret was his oldest sister, and I soon realized that she was my only support. I mustered up the courage to call her. There had been a telephone installed by the previous owner, so as soon as Keith went out the door, I picked up the phone and called my sister-in-law while in pure agony.

"Hi Margaret. Keith told me to call you."

"What's the matter?" she asked.

"I have really bad cramps in my belly." I gasped as another one hit so fiercely that I went to my knees. It was then that I realized what was actually happening. I was in labour!

A short time later, someone came by to bring me to a tiny plane waiting at the dock in Terrington Basin. I was immediately air lifted to the hospital at North West River, some thirty miles away. Through the agony of labour pains, I was admitted and wheeled to the birthing room. I was in labour for what seemed like hours, as the nurses and hospital staff kept me updated.

"How much longer, Miss?" I asked timidly. I felt uncomfortable with people in uniforms.

"Try to be patient, Josephine. It'll be a while yet," she replied.

Finally, after what seemed like forever, I was wheeled into the delivery room. The lights were blinding and I was in total agony. There was no epidural or any other type of medication to take at that time. I recalled being in St. Anthony Hospital in Newfoundland to have my tonsils removed and hearing blood-curdling screams from a distant room. In my curiosity I'd asked what was happening and was simply told, "Somebody's having a baby."

Now I could certainly understand why. Another thought came to me during my labour pains. I suddenly realized what my mother had endured. She had gone through labour fourteen times. I gained a new respect for her at that moment. She surely deserved it.

The following morning, on July 8, 1961, at 1:00 a.m., just eight days after we were married, our son made his way into this world. He weighed six pounds and eight ounces. Shortly afterward the nurse came into my room holding the most perfectly formed and tiniest bundle I'd ever seen.

I gingerly unswaddled him and checked all his fingers and toes. With tears of joy streaming down my face, I checked his tiny head and face and every part on his body. My baby, my very own baby! Oh, the joy of it! I named him Keith Gregory. I loved Gregory Peck, and we ended up calling him Gregory because I didn't want my son to be called Keith Junior or Junior.

At that time new mothers were kept in the hospital for seven days. During that time the hospital staff taught me how to care for him and breastfeed him and to burp him after each feeding.

"I know all that. I had a lot of brothers and sisters," I told the nurse.

"Oh, did you now? And how many did *you* have?"

"My mother gave birth to fourteen babies, but only ten of us survived."

"Wow! It must have been difficult for her," was all she said.

Keith didn't come to North West River to visit me while I was recovering, and I didn't expect him either. He was working and couldn't get the time off. The road leading to North West River was not yet paved and was in very bad condition. After seven days I was flown back to Happy Valley clutching my newborn in my arms.

Keith was beside himself with pride, but seemed to have trouble expressing it. However, it was evident as I laid our tiny baby on the bed how he felt. He sprawled onto the bed, scooped the tiny bundle into his hands, and stared at him for the longest time. *What is he thinking?* I wondered. By the look on his face, I could tell he was overwhelmed, as tears trickled down his cheeks.

Chapter 9

Trying to Adapt

So much had happened in little over a week that I couldn't think straight: getting married, living with Keith's parents, moving into a new house, a baby shower, and being rushed off to a strange place alone to have my baby! My mind was in turmoil. I was happy to be married, happy to have my own place. I was delighted with wee Gregory, and took great joy in bathing him each morning. I loved the smell of baby powder as I stuck my face into his tiny body now dressed in his new rompers. He was a good baby and hardly cried at all.

Three weeks into my marriage, after returning from the hospital in North West River, I was able to take stock of my situation and what I had to work with. I didn't have a bathroom. I didn't have a kitchen sink because there wasn't a sewer system on our street yet. I didn't have a washing machine, so I had to go next door and borrow Aunt Winnie's huge galvanized tub and scrub everything on the washboard as my mother had done. Oh, how I had hated that job, and I still hated it. Wanting to be a perfect wife and mother and having been taught to be responsible, I struggled to keep up. I'd just turned eighteen in January.

Back then there were two sizes of cloth diapers, long ones and square ones. I took pride in getting my baby's diapers as white a possible by bleaching them and adding "blueing" to make sure that when I hung them on the clothesline they would be perfectly white and without stains. Every garment had to be straight. All the long ones, then the square ones together, his sleepers and night gowns, tiny shirts, facecloths, and socks all had to be in order. When I brought everything in from the clothesline, I ironed everything. Even the hems of my bed sheets and flannel pyjamas. I could hear my mother and all the women I'd worked for in Cartwright echoing in my brain: "If you're gonna do a job, do it right."

Aside from caring for my newborn, I took pride in keeping my house clean. After scrubbing my floors on my hands and knees, I then added paste wax and polished the linoleum until it shone. We didn't have much furniture, only what came with the house. I was grateful for that, because we certainly couldn't afford to buy any. I grew up very poor, literally living from the American military dump, so that didn't bother me too much.

The only source of heat we had was a stove that burned wood and/ or oil. When the temperature during winter dipped way below zero we had to bundle up. I tried my best to keep the baby warm. However, when it got below minus twenty-five and minus thirty I worried about him freezing to death. It got so cold during the night that when I got up to check on him and pulled the covers down, his warm, wet body would meet with the cold air and the steam would billow up into my face.

Mrs. Penny would drop by every day to see how I was doing and to give me advice. She tried to show me how to care for my house and my baby. She didn't know that I grew up caring for my many siblings. I didn't want to be disrespectful to her; after all, she was my mother-in-law. I had to bite my tongue many times to stop from saying something I might later regret.

What had just happened to me? Where did my hopes and dreams of marrying a tall, dark, and handsome man go? Where did my freedom from responsibility go? Thankfully I was too busy to give it much thought. I never had a friend in the place and had to rely on my sisters-in-law for a lot of my needs. Sal went back home to Cartwright shortly after my wedding. My Aunt Winnie was a great help. I adored her. She had soft brown eyes that seemed to reach into her very soul.

Though I'm not sure to what degree, Aunt Winnie was living with a drinking man who occasionally abused her. I'd become too busy trying to adapt to my own situation, trying to cope with so many new things at once, to give it much thought. Now I was discovering the indifference of my husband. It was very unsettling.

Chapter 10

My First Job

Keith was working as a civilian for the Canadian Armed Forces when we got married. Therefore, we did have an income, but it wasn't enough to support us. There was so much to learn about finances. I hadn't yet experienced that aspect of my life. Aside from the two years as a cook at the mission school in Cartwright, the only thing I'd ever done was domestic work at ten dollars a month. I gave some of it to my mom for the children. Or to buy them candy. Keith came home from work one day and suggested I should find a job. I was awestruck. I had a job caring for our newborn and our home! Why would he even suggest it? A week or so later he came bounding through the door.

"I was talking to somebody today and he mentioned that there was an opening for a cashier at the PX on the American base."

"Whass a PX?"

"It's a store where the Americans shop," he said flippantly. As if I was supposed to know!

"So? What do you want me to do about it?" I asked, confused.

"Would you like to try it?"

"I don't know. I never did anything like that before. What will I have to do?"

"Just stack shelves and work the cash register and stuff," he replied.

I didn't know anything about cash registers, or store clerks, or stocking shelves. I didn't know how to express myself and was always fearful of ridicule. I was, however, taught to obey. Then fear engulfed me. I didn't want to leave my baby with strangers.

"Who will care for our baby?" I asked.

"We'll get somebody to come in," he said. "The money will come in handy for our new addition I want to build."

"What new addition? I like it just as it is," I argued.

"No, it'll be too small for us in a few years." Keith said.

I lost the argument and I hadn't any choice but to get someone to care for my three-month-old baby.

The very next day Keith drove me to the PX and I was hired on the spot. I can't recall how and I don't remember anything about an application or an interview. What was I to do? I didn't get much sleep that night. I had no decent clothes to wear and I had no idea what was in fashion. When I was younger my sisters and I would squabble over garments from the rag-bag of clothes mom got as payment for her sewing. When I was eleven years old I earned ten dollars a month as a domestic, and I was then able to order my own clothing from the Eaton's and the Simpsons-Sears catalogues. I prided myself in being one of best-dressed adolescents in my hometown. This was an entirely different situation. It required appropriate clothing and I was fearful my wardrobe would not measure up.

The next thing I remember, I was working in a huge department store for the American military. I didn't start cash right away. They put me to work stocking and reorganizing shelves. I was quite comfortable there because I knew I was a good worker and organizer. Also, I was very intrigued about all the different things the Americans had available to them; there were hundreds of products I had never seen before! I thought they were all millionaires. I had no concept of lifestyles, culture, hobbies, or theatre. I hadn't any concept of distance or space or anything about worldly goods and services that other human beings did. I was ignorant about everything.

They taught me how to count back change and I caught on quickly. I actually liked the challenge of it. I was then moved to the cashier's cage and enjoyed it very much. I had been conditioned from early childhood to always do a good job. So it didn't matter what I did, from that time on, my work ethics were hard-wired into my brain. It's not surprising then that I did well on the job. My superiors praised me for my work, and my chest filled with pride with the kind words they bestowed on me. I was enjoying this experience. Life was pretty good to this point.

I thought of my wee baby at home and felt terribly guilty for leaving him. He was such a good boy and easy to care for. My babysitter seemed to be doing well with him, which gave me a little relief.

The first New Year's Eve we experienced as a couple was a memorable one because I was too young to be permitted into the New Year's party. Here I was, married with a child, a home, and all the responsibilities that go along with that, yet not permitted to attend the Grand New Year's Eve Ball! I'd been hearing throughout the Christmas season that it was quite an occasion. Keith was so upset, and decided to do something about it. He went and visited the base commander. As a result, I got a special permit to attend.

I had never seen such hoopla in my entire life! There were fancy paper hats for everyone, lots of noisemakers, and in the ceiling there were hundreds of balloons tied into a mesh net. We had so much fun! Then at midnight all the balloons came floating down and everyone started hugging and kissing each other to the age-old song "Auld Lang Syne." I thoroughly enjoyed myself. I loved to dance, and by the end of the night I was exhausted, but happy to be a part of the adult world. I felt grown up. I was beginning to feel joy in being a responsible young wife and mother, with family and friends; a true part of our closely knit community. This new mindset however, was about to change.

Shortly afterward, in January of 1962, I missed my period for the third month. There was no mistaking it, I was pregnant again already. I didn't want another baby so soon. I was just beginning to settle into this new lifestyle; caring for my husband and baby son, enjoying my job and the challenges it gave me. But, I had to face the facts. Panic set in. Would I be like my mom and have thirteen children? Was there any way I could control the number of children I had? Was there any hope? However, I had to accept my plight and go on with my life. *I can do this,* I thought to myself. *I can find a way.... There has to be some form of birth control out here and I will find it.* In the meantime I would welcome this new baby with open arms. I brushed myself off and went back to work at the American military department store.

Then one day at work I was surrounded by several of the managing staff and told to report to the office.

"Josie, there seems to be a discrepancy in your cash."

"Pardon me?" I said, stunned. What the hell was discrepancy?

"There is fifty dollars missing from your cash that we can't account for and we have no choice but to let you go."

"But Miss, I didn't take any money. I swear!" I begged.

I could sense that I would get nowhere by begging and had no choice but to go home. I was shattered. The little confidence I had built in myself was gone and I shuffled around like a whipped puppy for days afterward. What had just happened? I knew I didn't take the money. I'd learned as a little girl the consequences of stealing. With my mother it was a cruel beating with whatever she could find: a huge back-hander, a belt, a willow, or a piece of backline. So I would never do that!

Once I arrived home I didn't know what to do with my anger. Normally it would take something drastic and over the top for me to lose all reason. I wasn't one to hit walls or throw things, but this time I lost it. I was not only angry, I was embarrassed, and hurt. My fundamental values had been questioned, and how would I tell my husband I was accused of stealing? I paced the floor. I couldn't breathe, all I could do was yell and scream. I was devastated. Keith felt so bad for me, but there was nothing he could do to ease my pain and frustration and that was that.

A few weeks later I got a phone call. On the other end of the phone was my boss from the PX.

"Josie, this is Gloria Hunt. It seems we have done you a grave injustice."

"What?"

"We found the fifty dollars that we blamed you for stealing and we are so very sorry."

Again, I was stunned and didn't know what to say.

"We were very pleased with your quality of work and with our humble apologies we would like you to come back to work!"

"Back where?" I mumbled, flabbergasted. I could feel my anger rising.

"Here at the store," she said so calmly that I wanted to shout and scream at her. I was losing it — again! I felt relief and sadness at the same time. I *knew* I hadn't stolen the money, I *knew* I was innocent, but was too stunned to say anything to her. All I said was, "I'm going to have a baby."

Chapter 11

Construction

It was spring in 1962. The first year of our marriage was, to say the least, overwhelming. It's probably a blessing that I was too busy to give it much thought. It was during that first winter that Keith decided to build a big addition onto our little house.

I was pregnant with our second child while our property was filled with tools, lumber, concrete, and all manner of building supplies. I hadn't seen any plans, and there'd been no conversations about Keith's decision to build an addition onto our home. I don't remember if we had the money or not. I didn't ask any questions. Nevertheless, as soon as the weather warmed up in April of that first year, the construction began.

I was beginning to get excited about the house. With the siding and roofing on, it looked huge! There wasn't any drywall on the walls. There weren't even any partitions up yet. There was a plywood floor and that was it for our new addition. I hadn't any idea what the rooms were going to be used for.

I had started a new job as a food service worker at the airport snack bar on the Canadian side near the runway. In this snack bar there were no waitresses. We prepared the food and served it from behind a long counter. I worked through the winter and into the summer until I had my second child.

In July there still wasn't a hospital in Happy Valley. A clinic on Hamilton River Road was the only medical service available in this somewhat pioneer town. At least for this baby I knew what was happening. When Keith dropped me off, I was in excruciating pain that seemed to go on for hours and hours. Near birthing time, Nurse Susan ordered me onto my side. I didn't understand. I had never heard of a side birth before. However, nothing was going to stop this feisty little infant from making her way into this world. Despite the unorthodox method used, Susan did a good job delivering my baby. On July 23, 1962, our first beautiful daughter was born. I didn't have a name for her at first. A few days later someone handed me a book of names. I searched through it and liked the sound of Darlene, I'd never heard it before growing up on the coast, so we named her Darlene Frances.

After one week I returned home with my newborn and placed her in her crib. She was fussy and seemed to be more demanding than her brother had been. She was the cutest baby from the start.

As soon as I was well enough I decided to go back to work. We would need the money to pay for materials for construction. I hired a babysitter for my children and started back at the airport restaurant. I worked all of that summer.

When he managed to squeeze time away from the club and his buddies, Keith continued to bang a few more nails into the house. In the meantime we got a dog. Every new family has to have a dog. It was the cutest Labrador retriever, with a shiny, jet black coat. We named her Tammy. She was a wonderful asset to our family and the children adored her. She was very gentle with the babies, and smart as well. It wasn't long before I had her trained to fetch, roll over, and so on.

Tammy grew fast and started having puppies, which added another burden to my life. Even though we enjoyed the experience of new puppies, I was the one stuck with all of the responsibilities of caring for them, such as cleaning up the messes and finding new homes for them.

My husband made a decision, somewhere along the way, that he didn't want the responsibilities of a family, and started not coming home after work. I was confused, because he'd been very supportive during my pregnancies up to this point.

"Where was ya?" I asked as he stumbled in the door.

"Just dropped in to have a few beers wit de boys after work," he slurred.

"Why?"

"Cause I wanted to."

"Well what about yer family?" I screamed.

And the fight was on. I was shocked and bewildered. I'd never seen him drunk before. He seemed to be angry about everything he'd ever done. But I didn't know what to do about it. What had I done to make him so angry?

Keith and I were trying desperately to earn a living, but we seemed to be going backwards. Would I be better off staying at home? Working five days a week required a nanny to care for the babies. We sat down one day to try and figure things out. We discovered that with the cost of two babies, new construction costs, heating and electricity costs, phone bills, grocery bills, and a nanny for the children, we were barely making ends meet. The problem was we didn't have a solution. I didn't have a clue how to manage money and I didn't know how to stand up for myself. All I could do was try.

"If only you'd come home after work instead of goin' to have a few beers wit de boys." I yelled. He didn't let me continue.

"Now wait a minute," he screamed, so loud it startled me. "I work hard every day on the job, and then I come home and work on the house."

I didn't hear anything else. I shut down. What was wrong with me? Why could I never win an argument? Why for once couldn't I be right? Why did I feel so rejected, dejected, and inferior to him? I didn't have the answerers and just gave up.

As the time passed Keith continued to stay out with the boys. I soon realized I would have to take charge of this household and focus on what I needed to do to care for our family. To feed and clothe my children, to make sure we paid the heating bills, so we wouldn't freeze to death in dead of winter, as the construction on the house remained unfinished.

Household Finance came to Goose Bay and opened up a branch just down the street from where we lived. We started hearing how easy it was to get money.

"What do you think? Should we go?" Keith asked as he returned home after work one day.

"I heard a lot of people get into trouble with those finance companies," I said, trying to sound educated.

"Well, maybe we can get a furnace for the house."

I liked the sound of that. It would be wonderful not to have to worry about firewood.

"But it will cost a lot more for fuel, won't it?" I asked.

After all was said and done, we decided to go for it. I put on my good clothes and we traipsed down the sandy road and knocked on the door. A smiling, vibrant young man shook our hands so hard it startled me. The place looked plush and professionally decorated with a shiny new desk and well-padded chairs. He motioned for us to sit down. I can't recall exactly what transpired, but the gist of it was that he was going to let us have a thousand dollars. Just like that! I didn't pay a lot of attention to the details. Besides, I didn't understand interest rates, or long-term payment plans, or cash advances. We left with more cash then we'd ever seen before. It was very tempting to splurge the money on things we didn't need.

After a short conversation we decided to go to the store and order a brand new furnace. We wanted to be smart and do the right thing. It would be wonderful when the cold weather came to not have steam billowing into my face from the babies' cribs as I lifted the covers off them.

There weren't any rocks in Happy Valley, which made it easy for digging the hole under the house to accommodate the new furnace. While we were waiting for it to arrive, Keith finished the digging and shored up the walls with plywood to protect the furnace and deter a sand slide. There wasn't any ductwork involved — just a hole in the ground. With help from his brother Graham and a friend, they installed our new furnace. One large grate placed in a corner of the living room finished the job. We had heat!

Chapter 12

Life Emergencies

In 1963 people were raving about the new hospital that just opened up in the Valley. When Darlene was six months old I started having weird sensations in my abdomen and decided to get them checked out. When I told them what was happening, they put me straight to bed. I was not informed why, and I wasn't even allowed to go to the bathroom. While using the bedpan, I felt a tiny bump leaving my body. The nurse came in to inform me that I'd just had a miscarriage.

"A miscarriage?" I didn't even know I was pregnant.

As I pondered about what had just happened, I cried. I stared at the tiny fetus in the bedpan and wondered what it might have been. Would it have been a boy or girl? Would it have been healthy or sick? What would I have called him or her? It was difficult to relate it to my two lovely babies at home. I allowed the tears to flow and grieved the loss of what could have been. After a few days, I was allowed to go home to my two healthy children. I hugged them as hard as I dared, and was grateful for them.

I ran to my Aunt Winnie next door and rested my head on her warm, soft shoulder and wept. I was so glad she was there. I hadn't heard from my family in months. Mom couldn't write very well; she had only a grade three education and didn't like to write. Brother Sammy didn't get to go to school at all. Marcie was married and had five children: four boys and one girl. One of her sons was stricken with cerebral palsy and couldn't walk, so she had little time to write. Sal was probably having relationship problems as well, as I hadn't heard from her since she returned to Cartwright after my wedding. It also seemed my sisters-in-law were much too busy to be bothered with me. Therefore, without my Aunt Winnie, I felt very much alone.

In the fall of 1963 I received an urgent call at work from my neighbour across the street.

"Josie, Gregie is hurt badly. Come home quick!"

"I'll be right there."

Terrible thoughts entered my mind as the old jalopy raced down the sandy road, dust billowing up behind so thick I couldn't see anything. I thought of how my mother must have felt when she landed on the stage head and saw something tragic had happened to her daughter!

Terrible memories of when I was two and a half engulfed me. My family lived a semi-nomadic life. Each fall we moved inland to my father's trapping grounds in Roaches Brook along with two other families. Each spring Dad moved his family back out to iceberg alley — Spotted Island in the North Atlantic — to harvest the rich cod fishing grounds. There was freedom to roam the rocky hillsides and play in the land wash. The husky dogs were also free to roam at will, free from harnesses and chains. They spent the summers gorging on fish and keeping cool underneath the houses that were built on stilts, as the ground was solid rock.

There was no store on the island and the sea roared constantly, so when it calmed down one day several island residents, including my mother, decided to go to Dawe's store across the run by boat to get food and supplies, leaving me in the care of Aunt Lucy. There was no communication in place back then, so there was no way for my mom to know what was happening to her child.

Being an inquisitive, free-spirited little girl, I wanted to see the new puppies that were born each spring, so I meandered next door with a piece of molasses bread in my hand. I fell down, and when I did the dogs saw this as an opportunity to get a morsel of food. They came racing to me and knocked me over onto my stomach. Then they proceeded to start eating my head! Once the other dogs heard the commotion, they joined in. Aunt Lucy heard the dogs snarling and came running out, her broom high in the air. She whacked the starving dogs away, but not before half the flesh was torn from the back of my head. The island residents of twenty-five families came running to the horrible scene. They grabbed me and wrapped me in a bed sheet, which was immediately red with blood.

"As soon as I climbed the stage head I knew something bad happened with the dogs; everyone was screaming and crying," Mom said. As soon as the boat landed, Mom came racing up the hill. Her worst nightmare had materialized!

"Everyone tried to stop me from seein' you, but they couldn't," she told me later.

"What did you do?" I asked.

"As soon as I took the sheet off and saw your little head, I fainted."

"What did you do to me then?" I stammered, horrified to hear my own story.

"When I came to, I took you in the house, boiled some juniper boughs and mixed them with bread to make a poultice, and wrapped it around your little head. I did that for three or four days until the steamer came and took you to the hospital in Cartwright. When you come home all you beautiful yellow ringlets were gone — just gone! And your new hair was growing out dark. It made me sad," she said, as once again, tears trickled down her cheeks.

As I too entered *this* terrible scene, I could certainly identify with my mother's horror. It's every mother's nightmare to witness a tragedy involving her child. As I approached the scene, I was horrified to see my little boy screaming in pain. I tried to stand him up. He fell to the ground with such an ear-piercing scream, it made my blood curdle. I checked him all over and when I lifted his pants leg his little leg was extremely swollen. I rushed to the clinic. Gregie had been playing with friends across the road when he either fell, or was pushed off a fire hydrant. The nurse took one look at him and sent us to the Canadian Forces hospital.

"It must be serious. It looks like it might even be broken!" the nurse said.

I cried as we sped up to the Canadian base and around the airport to the hospital located several miles on the edge of the forest. After a short examination the doctor gave us the terrible news.

"Gregory has a broken femur bone," he told us.

"What bone?" I managed to mumble. I hadn't any idea what he was talking about.

"Gregory has a broken thigh bone," the doctor explained after seeing the blank look on my face.

He went on to explain that, because it was a thigh bone, Gregory would have to stay in the hospital for several months. I couldn't tell him exactly how it happened because I'd been working at the time. It's hard to imagine that his thigh bone could break from falling off a fire hydrant into the sand, but that was the story I got and no one would say anything more about it. Keith came as soon as he'd heard and as we waited I tried to fill him in on what was happening. After the doctors had done their thing for what seemed like hours, they came out and told us we could go in to see him.

As we walked into the room my heart broke. There was poor little Gregory literally hanging upside down from a contraption made up of steel poles, tubes, and ropes. The doctor told us that because of the angle of the break, they couldn't put a cast on it. They had to hang him upside down to bring his thigh bone in line. His little backside was lifted off the bed. As if that wasn't bad enough, a couple of days later the doctors discovered that he kept kicking the broken leg with his good leg. They had no choice but to tie up his good leg as well. As I walked into the room day after day and saw my baby hanging like a hide of beef in a cold storage bin, my heart ached. However, we had no choice but to try to keep him occupied as much as possible. I would read to him, tell him stories, and bring him little toys he could play with on his chest. His life was suddenly so restricted. We were helpless to do anything for him. He spent a few months in the hospital, and we were very grateful that the Canadian military was able to do that for us. Gregory eventually healed and was able to come home. It was a great day when he joined his baby sister, who at that time was just two years old.

Chapter 13

Birth of a Town

During the Second World War, a refuelling station was needed on the east coast of Canada to service planes crossing back and forth from Europe. President Roosevelt's son, Captain Elliot Roosevelt and Dr. Forbes led the expedition, along with several local men, to search for the appropriate place to build an airport. They scouted Baffin Island and the Labrador coast. Eventually they came upon a huge parcel of land, well inland, and for the most part free of fog. It was located near Terrington Basin in Goose Bay. Equally as important, it was accessible by boat. Upon further investigation they discovered a huge plateau with sparsely covered trees caused by a forest fire in the area some thirty years earlier. It was all sand, with no rocks to blast through, so there would be minimal clearing necessary. One lady, who worked for McNamara Construction, got off the plane in the scorching heat wearing high heels. When her heels disappeared into the soft sand she was heard to say, "This can't be Labrador. We must be in a desert somewhere."

Once the decisions were made to use this site, the government didn't lose any time in getting the massive job of building an air base underway. Men were recruited from all across Canada, the United States, and the world. As Labrador was not yet part of Canada, they were told that because they were leaving the country of Canada they'd have to pay duty on any supplies purchased on site. Also, they would need to bring warm clothing. They were not allowed to talk to anyone about where they were going or why. It was top secret. Early construction workers suffered immense hardships the first few years working in inclement weather and mud up to their knees. Men from outside Labrador were paid fifty cents an hour while the local men were paid thirty-five cents an hour.

In Happy Valley, the first native Labradorians settled in Otter Creek. They erected crude tents and went to work for McNamara Construction. It was the main construction company hired to build Goose Bay. Otter Creek was the site allocated for fuel storage. After construction started all civilians were instructed to relocate as close to the base as possible. They found an ideal spot in a valley along a huge river called the Grand River, later renamed the Hamilton River and renamed again as the Churchill River, as it remains today. Shortly afterward, massive oil tanks were constructed in Otter Creek, adjacent to Terrington Basin and easily accessible to docking.

On September 26, 1943, three people, Gilbert Saunders from Davis Inlet, Thorwald Perrault-Makovik, and John Broomfield from Big Bay, arrived in what is now Happy Valley. They erected tents and started immediately to build the airport. Word spread that men were needed to work, and several days later Robert Davis and a couple more men moved in, and set up tents to work for McNamara Construction. It was first known as Refugee Cove, and then Skunk Hollow. Rumour has it that several airmen, lonely for entertainment, went searching for fun. After a night of playing cards and carousing with the locals, they returned to the base tired but happy. One of them is known to have said, "We had a good time in Happy Valley," so in 1955 a decision was made to rename it Happy Valley.

Mrs. Alice Perralt operated the first school from her home until 1946 when the Royal Canadian Air Force donated a building, which became the first one-room school house. In 1949, the military donated a second building and it became the first Anglican school, with fifty-three students.

When I arrived in July 1960, Happy Valley was fast becoming a vibrant community. In the beginning the Valley was made up of shacks built or constructed from leftover materials from buildings on the bases: either scavenged from sites or collected from the dump. As time went on, bigger and better homes were built. It was soon realized that a leader, a town manager, and a council would be needed.

There were new businesses cropping up all over town. Most were located along the main street of Hamilton River Road, which ran from the edge of town all the way to the dock in Terrington Basin. The Hudson's Bay store located at the end of Grand Street, which ran perpendicular from Hamilton River Road, was well established by the time I arrived in 1960. In1961, the first drug store, War's Pharmacy, was constructed just across the street from the Hudson's Bay store. The Grenfell Mission opened its first nursing station in 1951. Our first daughter was born there. In 1963, the provincial government built the Paddon Memorial Hospital. What a blessing that was! Our second daughter was born there in April 1964. In 1965 the water and sewer system was installed. Shortly after that the roads were paved. I'm not sure of the exact date, but the new town hall was constructed in late 1950s. Jim Finta opened up a new restaurant giving the long-running Saunders' Restaurant some needed competition.

A new golf course was built a few miles farther on the right side of the road. Keith helped clear the grounds for the fairways. He became one of the first golfers and a pioneer member of the club. Adjacent to the golf club, a second Hudson's Bay store serviced the Department of Transport area. Several other houses on Hamilton River Road completed that complex. It was later to be renamed Hamilton Heights.

All housing beyond the Valley was for military personnel and their families, along with civilian air traffic controllers and officials employed by DOT, until the amalgamation of the two locations. This caused a dramatic increase in the census. When I arrived in 1961, there were 2,861 people in the civilian census count, which doubled in 1966 to 4,215. By the time we left in 1977, Happy Valley–Goose Bay, along with the newly amalgamated communities of Spruce Park and Hamilton Heights, reached approximately 7,000 people. There seems to be conflicting figures regarding the true population of the area after the amalgamation of *all* the areas of Happy Valley–Goose Bay. One report states 14,000 inhabitants in the mid 1970s.

Hamilton River Road was the only road that ran through the whole area of Happy Valley–Goose Bay. It started on the Hamilton River (now known as the Churchill River) at Buck's Landing. Buck Michelin was a pioneer who'd lived on the river for many years. Hamilton River Road followed the river eastward through Happy Valley on a northern angle, then elbowed right, just under the "bench" or hill leading to Department of Transport (DOT) area, later to be known as Hamilton Heights. It then flowed east through the DOT housing complex. Another couple of miles along Hamilton River Road leads to the only junction, which runs perpendicular, northward to the American base. This junction became a focal point for the community because it had a gas station and garage. From the junction Hamilton River Road carried onward through to the Spruce Park area where there were a couple of housing complexes. It then continued several more miles to the Canadian military base. Just past the base it crested at the hill and ran down on a southeast angle to the docks in Terrington Basin.

The American base with its gigantic aerodromes was located about a mile from the junction. It was off-limits to anyone without the proper identification. The United States Armed Forces checkpoints had been installed from the beginning to keep the military men confined to the base and the civilians out. Anyone working on base was supplied with identification cards. Most Labradorians did not like the checkpoints. For centuries they'd been free to roam their massive land, hunting and trapping. For centuries it had been their only means of survival. Therefore, they felt very confined once they entered the stringently controlled military sites and checkpoints.

The American base was a mystery to us. In the event we entered it, we immediately felt alien. Once through the checkpoint, to the immediate right were the massive aerodromes and runways. I was always in awe of the mighty British aircraft the Avro Vulcan XL361 jet fighters and the British Panavia Tornados parked along the perimeter of the aerodrome.

They stretched from the checkpoint to the treeline, several miles away. From the junction along Hamilton River Road on the south side was the post office and Bell Canada building.

At the corner on the left side of Hamilton River Road leading into Spruce Park stood the Royal Bank and a variety store. This complex contained several styles of housing: single-family bungalows, two-storey single-family dwellings, and steel structured units called Steelocks. They were single-storey duplexes with solid steel siding and ten-foot-high ceilings. All the housing was very comfortable and furnished with modern furniture. Spruce Park also had a school and a store. Across Hamilton River Road in the Spruce Park area, residents had the convenience of a large co-op store and a barber shop. Leaving Spruce Park, the road continued down the hill to another fork: one led to Terrington Basin where all the docking and shipping facilities were located. The Hamilton River Road continued on to the community of North West River some twenty-five miles away.

There were lots of clubs in Goose Bay. Both bases had a club for each rank. We were civilians, so Keith and I started going to the Department of National Defence's club we called the DND club, until the Squirrel Club opened up, which was the only civilian club on the Canadian side. Every Saturday night I got to dress up for the dance. There was always a live band made up of local musicians playing the latest country music, and I loved to dance. Keith, on the other hand, liked to drink. Sometimes if he thought I was getting too friendly with a person I'd been dancing with he would start a ruckus.

In the Valley, plenty of new buildings were going up and old shacks were being replaced with nice new homes as people could afford them. Labradorians helped one another as they had helped my father when he'd built our tiny house in Cartwright in 1953. There were new churches being built, new schools, and several new stores constructed. A brand new town was coming into being, and I was happy to have been a part of it all.

Chapter 14

New Neighbours

What was life all about? How did I end up in an abusive marriage? Was I not smart enough to see what was coming? I didn't know the answer to any of these questions. All I can say at this point is that I was trapped with two small children. The only place I felt comfortable and safe was at work. Work had become my only sanctuary.

Keith's parents were very old and his father had the whitest hair I'd ever seen. He always wore a sports jacket, and every day he would drop by and have the children search his jacket pockets for candy. He was a nice man and never said anything demeaning to me. I never felt judged by him. It wasn't quite the same with Keith's mom. She never came right out and said anything mean to me, but I could tell she didn't respect me. She didn't seem to have confidence that I could take care of my family. I tried so hard to get a compliment from her. I kept my house tidy and scrubbed the linoleum floor so hard that I rubbed the finish off, exposing the brown underneath. I was obsessive with my household duties. I knew how to keep a house. I had been doing it all my life! However, Mrs. Penny had no way of knowing this, because I couldn't bring myself to talk to her. I was too afraid. It certainly didn't help matters any when one day I'd done something that impressed her and she said, "I guess you're good for *something*, I suppose." I felt like crawling under the table.

I came home from work one day and there was a new foundation being built just one house down from ours. I went to my Aunt Winnie's next door and asked her if she knew who it was.

"Tis Murray Pardy, I think," she said matter-of-factly.

"What? Murray Pardy? It can't be."

Sure enough, it was Murray building his house, almost on my doorstep!

"But why?" I asked my Aunt Winnie.

She knew of my past and had been a great help to me early on in my marriage and settling into the community. Suddenly I was frightened. I was bewildered and confused. He was married to a lady named Shirley and had his own family. Even though we had parted amicably and he hadn't bothered me in any way, I felt there had to be a reason for him to build next door to us.

There was also another concern: Keith was an insecure and jealous man. How would they get along? I became very upset at this situation. It was extremely unnerving indeed!

"Did you know he was gonna build there?" Keith asked as he slammed his coat in a chair.

"No I didn't," I said.

"Then what the fuck is going on?" he screamed.

"Nothin' is goin' on. Murray and I have been through since the day I met you, Keith. You have to believe that."

"I don't know what to believe anymore!" he shouted.

"He hasn't bothered me in any way," I yelled.

I was telling the truth, but Keith wouldn't believe me. We were in a standoff and unable to do anything about it. I couldn't stop thinking about why Murray would do this. Did he still love me to the point that just being beside me would be enough? Did he know Keith was jealous and could get very violent when he drank too much? Was he trying to break up my marriage? Moreover, what about his own family? Did he love them? He had a nice wife and beautiful babies. Did Shirley know that we had been lovers for years? There were so many questions milling around in my head. I didn't need this burden on top of everything else!

Murray finished his house and moved his family in. At first I didn't become friends with Shirley. We stayed away from each other as much as possible. We were not mean to each other, just indifferent. We were both very busy working and raising our children. The whole situation made me feel uneasy. Not to mention how it must have made Keith feel. Given the uncomfortable circumstances, and all things considered, I thought he handled it pretty well. As far as Murray was concerned we just ignored each other. Shirley kept him in check. What could possibly happen next?

Chapter 15

My First Friend

By the summer of 1963 I was busy working at the restaurant and caring for my two small children. What was happening to Keith? He never came directly home after work. Many times he would come home late for supper and I would probably have it saved in the oven for him. Sometimes he would stay out until the club closed down; there were times when I would get so angry I didn't care what he did to me.

The first physical fight happened one night when he was late coming home. He was really drunk and staggering. He came to the door and asked me to put the children to bed. He didn't want them to see him in such a drunken state. So, with much complaining from them, they stomped off to bed. He then stumbled inside and sat at the kitchen table. As a rule I would have his supper in the oven. This night I took his supper out of the oven, placed it in front of his nose, and then dumped it in the trash can. *Smack!* The first blow struck my face so hard it almost knocked me over.

"What the fuck did ya do that for?" he screamed.

"Cause I'm sick an' tired of you coming home drunk every night and thinking yer gonna get yer supper or whatever else you think yer entitled to!" I screamed.

"I'm starvin'. Now what am I gonna eat?"

"I don't care if you never eat another bite as long as you live. You shudda thought a that hours ago."

He continued to hit me and I ran to the bedroom in case the children might see what was happening. He kept beating me and we struggled like two wild cats until he tired himself out or passed out; I'm not sure which. I was beside myself with sadness and felt trapped in a situation I couldn't escape from. Fear, as never before, engulfed me. There had been no evidence of violence before we were married. I suddenly realized that I was married to a very dangerous man. Furthermore, I felt helpless to do anything about it.

The following morning when Keith saw my bruised and battered body he was beside himself with grief. He dropped to his knees, placed his head in my lap, and wept. As I caressed his head with my hands, I tried to figure him out. However, it was beyond my comprehension. How could a person have such totally opposite sides to him? If he loved me how could he be so cruel?

"Oh, Josie, please, please forgive me," he begged.

I was speechless. It tore me up inside to see him suffer this way. *He must love me then,* I thought.

On Friday night Keith came home in time for supper. "Would you like to go to the dance Saturday night?" he asked. "Joe English is playing."

"Oh ya. I love Joe English's band."

So, on the weekend we got all dressed up. By this time I was old enough to get into the DND club and I loved it! Being a dancer and music lover from way back as a small child I was thrilled to go to the Saturday night dance.

After greeting a few friends and getting settled in our seats, I looked around to see if anyone new had arrived in town. Being a transient base, people moved in and out constantly. I spotted this beautiful woman with long brown hair sitting a few tables away. I couldn't stop looking at her. She was the prettiest woman I'd ever seen! Finally, in the washroom later that evening we introduced ourselves.

"I'm Josie Penny, Keith's wife. He's the loud one," I managed to say. I was not accustomed to being the person to make the first move. However, I was lonely and I knew I needed a friend. I hadn't made one to this point.

"I'm Melanie, but everybody just calls me Emcee."

It sounded like a strange name; not a Labrador name that I was familiar with.

"You talk different than us. Where are you from?" I asked.

"Inverness, Nova Scotia," she said.

I had no idea where Inverness was or even Nova Scotia either, other than that it was a province of Canada. Suddenly I felt as I'd felt long ago when we moved to Cartwright and I thought all the "up the harbour" people were so much better than us. I couldn't be friends with someone so pretty and educated, especially from a place called Nova Scotia!

"Have you been here long?" she asked me with a distinct Canadian accent. She sounded like the military people and she sounded nice and she seemed interested in me. What should I do, talk to her or run? We did talk and we became life-long friends.

It wasn't long after meeting Emcee and her husband Raymond that we met other people. Raymond was a mechanic and worked in the motor pool with a bunch of guys: George Cluney, Ned Duggan, Dave Whitten, and several others. They were civilians from Newfoundland. There were several Labrador men there as well: Jim Saunders, John Crane, Gerald Bird, Don Saunders, and others. After meeting and chatting with their wives at the club several times, all of us became friends and partied together almost every weekend for several years. We had so much fun! As a young woman from Cartwright without a sense of place or belonging, it was difficult to believe deep down inside me that anyone could like me or accept me as a friend.

Keith was very funny, and even though he was shy at first, he became the trickster — after a few drinks of course. They would pull stunts and tricks on each other at work and during our house parties. We laughed at the goings-on of these grown men acting like children. For the time being, and to some degree, we had fun. It relieved stress and it was something I had to tolerate or pay the consequences for. I became very busy with work, my children, and my new friends.

I received a pleasant surprise one day in late summer of 1963. My sister Rhoda came to live in Happy Valley. She was only sixteen, but had been working as a nurse's aide in Cartwright for a few years. Then she was transferred to the newer and much larger hospital in North West River, only thirty miles from the Valley. It was wonderful to see her, but I didn't know her very well. I hadn't spent enough time with my parents when my siblings were little to get to know them. I do remember her having nose bleeds so bad that mom had to hold a bucket under her to catch it all. It left her weak and sickly. When she walked through my door I didn't know her! She was very tall, slim, and beautiful. So, even though Keith was not a supportive husband and went about his life as he saw fit, I, at least, had one friend and now one sister near me.

Chapter 16

Struggling to Cope

My new friend Emcee and I became good friends. In the fall of 1963, I discovered I was pregnant again. We were at the club one night when she told me she was pregnant with her first child.

"Really? So am I! When are you due?" I asked.

"In the spring, around April or May," she replied.

"That's when I'm due as well!"

We were delighted to both be pregnant at the same time, but I was scared. What would I do with another baby? I was barely keeping up with the two I had! Although they were adorable and played happily together, I was overwhelmed. I made sure they were fed, although it became increasingly difficult to scrape up enough money for good food. I was conscientious enough about their health to get them outside each day for exercise and fresh air.

The odd time when Keith did manage to make it home before their bedtime, he would wrestle on the floor with them. He had never changed a diaper or fed them or had anything to do with them as tiny infants, but he enjoyed roughhousing with them when they got a little bigger.

"I'm afraid I'll break 'em," he'd say.

Was it because he didn't know how? After all, he'd been the youngest of his family and had never been around babies in his life. Keith's youngest sibling was nine when he was born, so he knew nothing about infants.

The children loved to see their grandfather come by with candies in his pocket. Mrs. Penny, on the other hand, would sit around and try to tell me what to do or how to run my household. I was pleasant with her and took it all in stride. She was so old anyway it didn't feel right to argue with her. Keith's brother Graham had built a house for them just around the corner, so they were close by.

One night we were acting like a normal family and having supper when we heard a ruckus outside. We jumped up from the table and raced to the door. There was Graham, loaded drunk and fighting with somebody. It was our neighbour Ralph, Aunt Winnie's oldest son who lived on the other side of us. They were on the ground. Keith rushed out, grabbed his brother, and tried to reason with him. It was quite the struggle because both men had brute strength and were out of control. I don't recall why or what caused it. I was disturbed that yet another drunk was causing me grief. Was there no end to the madness?

We lived on Grand Street, and if you looked out my front window or exited my front door you would be looking straight down Markland Road. Dorcass lived just down Markland Road on the right. At least a couple times a week I saw Dorcass, Margaret, and Mrs. Penny walk arm-in-arm past my house, around the corner, and head for Dorcass's place for their afternoon tea. I was never once invited. Although I am sure it was unintended, I felt belittled, inferior, and sad. I felt that they didn't like me or I wasn't good enough for them. It certainly added to the feelings of inferiority that I'd carried with me all of my life.

I was in desperate need of support. I wanted someone to love me. I'd been convinced that Keith didn't love me and that I was just a convenience to him. It breaks my heart to even think about it, but after losing my third baby in an early miscarriage, I thought that maybe, just maybe I could cause another one. In fits of anger and despair I pounded my swollen belly. I cursed my situation, then in shame and emotionally broken I sank

Gregory with his dad and grandparents, Elsie and Mark Penny in the house under renovation on Grand Street, 1964.

to the floor and wept. How did I get in this situation? What had happened to my dreams? Had I any dreams? I felt desperate and didn't know what to do. I did love my children, I just didn't think I could manage another one.

April 20, 1964, in a brand new hospital that had recently opened, my second beautiful daughter, Catherine Elsie, came into the world. She was slightly underweight, at five pounds, two ounces. I was afraid she was going to break. The doctor allowed me to take her home anyway. When I placed her on the bed, Keith sprawled beside her and checked her all over. I could see the look of pride on his face, but he was a man of few words. Suddenly he spoke.

"Her little legs are the same size as my finger," he mumbled, as much to himself as to me.

"Oh yah," I said as I nuzzled down beside them on the bed. I checked her all over and discovered that her tiny legs were indeed the same size as his fingers. "She's a wee little thing, isn't she?" I marvelled, happy in the moment.

Those special moments were few and far between. They gave me a little hope that things might get better.

I struggled and fought to try to get my baby to drink her formula, but all she wanted to do was sleep. After a few weeks I could see that she wasn't gaining any weight, so we went off to the hospital again to find out what the problem was. They decided to keep her in the hospital for several weeks until she reached six pounds. I was happy when we were allowed to take her home again. Even though it was difficult to get her to wake up and eat, she finally started to gain weight and thrived. She was so beautiful, and each time I thought of what I had almost done to this precious baby in my times of doubt, sorrow, fears, and pain, I flinched and cried in shame. She grew rapidly and developed the most amazingly doll-like face, and she was such a smiling happy baby!

The Penny family in the house on Grand Street in 1965. Note the floors. L-R: Darlene (age two), Josie, Gregory (age three), and Keith.

The summer of 1964, my sister Sal, just one year younger than me, came to visit with her baby son, Steven. He was the same age as Cathy, so I was delighted. The first thing we noticed was the difference in their weight and shape. Cathy had rosy apple cheeks and Steven was thin with long arms and legs.

When Cathy was six months old and doing well I decided to go back to work. I had to because Keith was not bringing his meagre earnings home. I didn't know why, and I had to find out. When he came home very late and drunk one night, I was ready to confront him.

"Where's all the money goin'?" I hollered.

"None of yer fuckin' business," he screamed back.

"It *is* my business. You have a family to feed," I cried. "How can you be so selfish and immature?" I had bruised his ego. The blows came again and again, knocking me to the floor. I was helpless against his brutality.

I found out later that he was not only drinking but gambling as well. In order to keep us from starving I had to hire another babysitter and return to work at the airport restaurant. I was grateful for my working skills. It was a busy place. I enjoyed working as my favourite songs filtered through the stereo system. I served my customers with as much enthusiasm, dedication, and false happiness as I could muster.

I didn't ask for much. I was fairly easy-going and at times Keith could be very loving and tender. During those precious moments he could convince me of anything. He could be a great family man once he stayed sober long enough to realize what he might be missing.

I enjoyed my family when I wasn't working. I would make sure they got fresh air every day. I couldn't get out often in the dead of winter during January and February, but once March came it was warm enough to take them outdoors. One winter's day I bundled up the kids for Keith to take them on a family drive while I had to work. We had an old jalopy we'd picked up from Carl Gruber's Garage. There were no seatbelts in the car. The kids were all bundled up in their winter suits. Cathy was wearing a pink snowsuit handed down to her from her big sister. They were on their way up the hill to the transmitter site when the door opened and Cathy fell out! Then it closed softly. The other kids didn't say anything or if they did Keith didn't hear them. No one knows *what* exactly happened.

Keith was unaware that Cathy and fallen out the door and had kept on driving! Thank goodness she hadn't slipped under the wheels because there were high snow banks from the snowplough all along both sides of the road. I will be forever grateful that a friend we knew was driving behind and picked Cathy up. He tried to get Keith's attention, but got no response. He then followed Keith all the way home. Keith was shocked to see the man in his driveway holding Cathy in his arms. After that we made sure the car doors were always locked.

I think at this time it's safe to say that at age twenty-one, with three children under four, a drunken, absent husband, a half-built shack, a dog with puppies running wild through the house, and no one to support me, I felt very much alone.

Keith's parents in front of our house on Grand Street, 1965. Back row, L-R: Mark Senior and Keith; Front row, L-R: Elsie, Cathy, Darlene, and Gregory.

Chapter 17

A Growing Community

In the summer of 1965, I was struggling to bring water from next door one day when huge diggers appeared on our sandy road. They were finally digging to put the water and sewer system in! It was an easy dig. This was a community built on sand. Since there were no rocks, it didn't take them long to have huge open pits in front of our house. I could only imagine how relieved the workers must have been, not having to contend with huge rocks and heavy boulders in the ground. I was concerned that there were no barriers around them. I took photographs of my children standing on the humongous mounds of sand in front of our home. Although sand was cleaner than mud, on rainy days it stuck to your boots and there wasn't any escape from it. When the wind blew, so did the sand. It was everywhere!

The following year the roads were finally being paved. Although grateful this time had finally come, we had to deal with the heavy equipment once again. It took most of the summer. The most annoying thing about that job was the odour from the tar, or whatever they used. Even so, it was a pleasure to have a little less sand blowing into the house every time the door opened.

I was also very pleased that our town finally had a hospital. The spanking new building on the corner of Grenfell and Hamilton River Road stood out. Across the street from the hospital, Father Charlie of the Roman Catholic Church oversaw the construction of a huge complex of buildings: the church, a school, and a residence. He seemed to be well-known and loved. I was not familiar with any of that as I did not attend any of the new churches that were popping up throughout the community. One of the biggest beatings I got from my mother as an adolescent was when I went to my friend's house to play cards on Sunday night instead of going to church. Had I now become an atheist? I can't answer that question; I just knew I didn't want anything to do with churches. I had attended church a few times when Keith and I were courting, primarily because Keith's father was heavily involved in the church. In earlier times he had been a lay reader or catechist in the Anglican Church in Battle Harbour, Labrador. There were many tales of "immense hardship" and "close calls for survival," as he put it, when travelling by dog team to service the spiritually starved people of Labrador's vast coastline.

In the following years, newer houses were built with store-bought lumber and materials, giving the once run-down community a far cleaner look. Residents started to build gardens and grow lovely green lawns. All they had to do was clear away the debris and sprinkle grass seed. It grew well in the sandy soil. More meticulous people had different soils mixed in to give the ground more substance.

The main department store was the Hudson's Bay store on Hamilton River Road. Another store located on Court Manche Road was in direct competition with Hudson's Bay. It was owned by Reginald Snelgrove. Keith had actually worked for him there for a short time before he met me. My sister-in-law Margaret ran a new clothing store simply called The Family Store. I taught her how to drive her new Volkswagen Beetle.

Adding new streets and paving them was an ongoing event in those early years. There was also a car dealership. Labrador Motors had been up and running for several years before I arrived in Happy Valley. The owner was Mr. Karl Gruber from Germany. His top mechanic, Martin, also from Germany, was a nice man and won the hearts of many people.

There wasn't any competition and very little chance for bartering. To this day we probably will never know if the prices of goods and services were fair, inflated, or gouged. We had nothing to compare them to.

Most homes were heated with fuel and wood. Melvin Woodward from Newfoundland owned the fuel oil company and delivered fuel to our homes when needed. He lived directly next door to Margaret on Cabot Crescent. There were many times when we needed fuel and hadn't any money to pay for it. We had to do without and try to scrape up enough wood to keep from freezing. I was thankful that our stove could burn both oil and wood.

There were new businesses cropping up all around the Valley. Three miles up the plateau on the Hamilton River Road in the Ministry of Transport area a small mini mall similar to a corner store was owned by Herb Brett. In previous years it had been a small hotel used by transient workers and construction workers, until the Labrador Inn was built just down the road. The mini mall, as it was called by the local residents, was located between two housing complexes, Hamilton Heights and Spruce Park, and serviced the residents in those areas. They no longer had to travel all the way to the Valley. Finally there was additional competition with the Hudson's Bay and Snelgrove's store. Shortly afterward Herb started the first ever local newspaper, *The Northern Reporter.* It was exciting to see what was happening. There weren't any computers of course; everything was typed out on legal sized paper and stapled together. At least it was our own paper and our own local news.

So the tiny makeshift village was quickly becoming a well-organized and friendly community with all the amenities one needs to live a fairly productive life. The franchises established in the mid-sixties elsewhere hadn't arrived in Goose Bay. There weren't any hair salons, and I'd never heard of a pedicurist or manicurist. Bert the barber had a barbershop on the Canadian side, just down Hamilton River Road from the Canadian Forces base. With all the military men and civilians working, he did well.

The diverse population of Happy Valley was made up of many nationalities from many different areas of the country and the world.

The different clubs on base were the rallying point for all civilian citizens. Non-military members and civilians were not permitted on base unless you had a special invitation or escort. We became very familiar within in a very short time with guards and military police. We had to always bring our identification cards, which were issued when we started work. Other than at work, we were segregated from all military activities: from the stores that sold all types of merchandise, from snack bars that sold good food, from theatres, and from clubs. Whether intentional or otherwise, we felt inferior. It had become our way of life.

Chapter 18

Moving

In September 1965, I was working in the mess hall on the Canadian side. I had hired a full-time housekeeper to care for the children. Keith was still doing his thing, so I had to take charge of everything. I discovered I was pregnant — again. I was *not* happy because we already had three babies under five years old: Greg was four, Darlene was three, and Cathy was just seventeen months old. Once again I thought of my mother and how she must have felt when she was expecting her fourth, her eighth, and her twelfth. There must be some form of birth control out there. If so, after this baby I would find it.

There was no stopping this baby once the time came. On April 7, 1966, I started having cramps, followed by two more in quick succession. By now I knew what was happening. This baby wanted to enter this world fast! I phoned Keith and he rushed me to the hospital. In just three hours, our son Mark was born. He was our biggest baby, at seven pounds, fourteen ounces. He was healthy and strong with blond hair and big blue eyes. He was adorable.

Mark's first birthday, April 1967. Sitting at the table and chair set their dad had made for them: L-R: Cathy, Josie, Darlene, Gregory, Mark, Keith, and Sal's son, Steven.

I bounced back quickly after having my babies. Shortly afterward I went to the doctor and we talked about some form of birth control. I surely needed something because I kept getting pregnant. I had four babies by the time I was twenty-four.

I had many things to be grateful for during this time in my life: I was strong physically, and due to my childhood experiences I knew how to care for small children; I knew how to run a household and was efficient at my jobs; and I'd learned a lot about healthy living and the importance of good food and fresh air. With those skills in place and my instinctive nature, I was able to manage my family very well. In terms of feelings, though I loved my children as much as any mother possibly could, I often wondered if I was capable of showing them enough love and attention to fill their needs. Something deep inside me told me "no."

About that time in Happy Valley local officials insisted that all residents had to move off Birch Island. It was a tiny, sandy island in the river that our earliest settlers had inhabited in the 1940s. The local government was looking for properties to relocate the Birch Island residents. Keith, in his infinite wisdom, saw it as a way to get immediate, much-needed cash. He sold our house on Grand Street for seven hundred dollars. He never did finish it and he didn't even bother to tell me he was going to sell it.

Suddenly, we were being moved to a tiny house on Hamilton River Road owned by Mr. Dalton. I had no idea what Keith had planned for us. I just knew we were to rent it while Keith looked for some land to build us a new house. It was so small it looked like it could have been used as his garage. I appreciated the location because we were just across the road from the river. Even though I worried about the children falling off the bank into the river or getting hit by a car because we were close to the busiest road in town, I enjoyed the close proximity to the stores and the wild raspberries that grew in abundance along the river bank. Also, the view of the river and being close to the water soothed my soul.

There was another large river about ten miles from Happy Valley called Goose River. It was fast and at times could be very dangerous, but it had a fabulous sandy beach with an area of slow moving waters suitable for swimming. We liked taking the children there to swim during hot summers.

My new friend Emcee and I would take our babies to different places in their strollers. We loved each other's company and I was grateful to her for being there for me. She would tell me how it had been living in Inverness and I was fascinated. I was feeling happy! I was learning to cope with Keith's antics to some degree and we were enjoying the company of friends.

In July 1966, Keith and I, along with our baby, Mark, who was three months old, and with the help of funds from the sale of our house, took a little trip to Newfoundland to visit Keith's sister Mabel. She lived in Corner Brook on the west coast of the island. At the time it was Newfoundland's second largest city, and was supported by the largest paper mill in the province. I was so excited, but worried about leaving the other three children behind. My sister Sal, who was living with us at the time, offered to care for the children. I knew she was very capable and I trusted her.

As we flew across the Strait of Belle Isle in the tiny de Havilland Otter my spirits lifted. The giant icebergs were in sharp contrast to the navy blue of the North Atlantic as they made their way south into infinity. It's what they'd been doing for the duration of time. We landed in Deer Lake and had to drive through mountains that bordered the great Humber River. I was in awe. I'd never seen such beauty! I was totally flabbergasted with the vastness of the mountains we had to drive through.

"Can you see the man in the mountain?" Keith asked as we slowed down to look.

"No, I can't find it," I said, as my eyes searched the huge mountain face.

So we pulled off to look. Sure enough, it was so plain that you'd think somebody had carved it into the face of the mountain. I was informed that many years ago a piece of the mountain wall had fallen away and left the shape of a human head in a pointed hood. I could clearly see it had a pointed nose, shaded eyes, a mouth, and a chin. This feature in such an awesome mountain wall intrigued me and captured my spirit. The great Humber River flowed gently along the bottom of the mountain, adding to the beauty all around me.

We made our way around the mountain, which followed the Humber River and into Corner Brook. It was the first time I'd ever seen a city. I was impressed with the size of Corner Brook and its awesome location. It was nestled into, around, and between massive hills. All the streets were paved and giant trees lined both sides. There were sidewalks with immaculately manicured lawns and well-kept gardens filled with beautiful flowers everywhere. I was awestruck. Other than being in St. Anthony Hospital when I was fifteen, I hadn't seen much of the outside world. Everything was so orderly and clean.

Mabel took us to Bowater Park. Our son was too young to enjoy the experience but I certainly did. There were statues of Smokey the Bear to remind visitors of the dangers of smoking in the park. We went swimming at the beach, and again I was impressed with the cleanliness of the beach. That evening Keith took me to see my first train down at the train station. The tracks for the *Newfie Bullet*, as it was affectionately called, were narrower than the trains of mainland Canada, but they were adequate for Newfoundland. We sat on the side of this huge hill and watched them roar by.

Mabel showed us a wonderful time. I was mystified as Keith pointed out where he used to hang out with his buddies. All too soon it was time to go home, and even though I thoroughly enjoyed the holiday I was happy to get back to the rest of our family. The children were happy to see their mommy and daddy. I went back to work and things returned to normal.

During the summer of 1966, Keith came bounding in the door one day.

"I finally got a piece a land and I'm gonna build us a new house," he said as he threw his coat in the corner.

"What? Where to?" I asked.

"Cabot Crescent," he replied matter-of-factly, as if he was going to the store.

With a growing family we certainly needed something, but I had my doubts. It was a relief to see him go ahead with his plans, a plan that I didn't know existed, which was that if he could get the land he wanted, he would build us a new house. Therefore, when the town started allotting plots of land on Cabot Crescent to residents at no cost, Keith jumped at the chance and applied for it. Keith was true to his word this time and soon afterward the bulldozer was there, digging out the basement.

He started building a huge house with a full basement. For once Keith seemed to really make an effort to take care of his family. He started out with great enthusiasm. All that summer of 1966 he worked at pouring the basement and putting up the walls of our new house. I was starting to get excited! Keith was working hard on trying to get our house ready to move into before the cold weather set in.

In the meantime, I was really beginning to enjoy the location of the tiny hut on Hamilton River Road. The Hudson's Bay store was just down the road and I could pick wild raspberries all along the riverbank. I loved to pick berries. It had been ingrained in me since early childhood.

The little house we'd been renting had a huge two-hundred-gallon fuel tank located next to the front steps. It was sitting in a wooden cradle and was actually touching the house. One day our oldest son Gregory, who was five at the time, came upon a box of matches. He wanted to light a fire, so he did. He even had the wherewithal to collect a huge wad of paper to light it with. Soon afterward, I could smell something burning and couldn't find the source. Then I saw smoke coming in the door. I ran outside and was horrified — there was a fire under the fuel tank! Thank goodness we caught it in time before the flames heated the tank enough to explode. As a result of that incident, we were asked to move. We'd been evicted!

I didn't know what evicted meant. I'd never heard of it before. I didn't know that one human being could do that to another human being. Where I came from on the coast of Labrador, if someone didn't have a place to live, someone else just took them in. No questions asked. We had no place else to go! Then Keith got a brilliant idea.

"Why don't we move into our own house?"

"What do you mean? It's not even half done!"

"I know, but I can get the basement done. It's got an eight-foot-high ceiling, and once I get the roof on and the main floor closed in, we'll have lots of room in the basement."

"What? You mean we gotta move into it like that?"

"Ya, and I can finish the upstairs before the summer."

I couldn't believe what he was saying! He meant it. We were going to have to move into the basement for the winter. What was wrong with me? Why couldn't I have insisted that we find another house? Why and how could I possibly allow this to happen?

Keith had to work long hours to enclose the main floor of the house before we moved in. He didn't get a chance to put windows in, so he barred them up and focused on putting the partitions in the basement. The wall joists were still bare inside the house. He put up drywall to separate the kitchen from the two bedrooms, on one side only, without insulation, windows, or doors. The stairs led up to the only escape route, the exit door on the main floor. Electricity was the only source of light. The only thing to brighten up the basement was the red and white linoleum floors, which after a few months turned brown as the shiny new top was worn away. It became very unsightly and impossible to keep clean. The one big room served as kitchen and living room.

In the fall of 1966, with frost heavy on the ground, we moved into the basement of our new house. Eight of us crammed into this hole in the ground, without sufficient heat to keep us warm. With the exception of a toilet, there was no indoor plumbing. There was nowhere near enough space to accommodate us: there was Keith, myself, five-year-old Gregory, four-year-old Darlene, two-year-old Cathy, and our six-month-old baby Mark, plus my sister Sal and her two-year-old son Steven. In 1964, when Steven was three months, Sal came to Happy Valley for a short visit. She then returned to Cartwright for a few years. When Steven was two years old in the summer of 1966, Sal came to Happy Valley because she was a single mom and had no place else to go. It couldn't have worked out better for the both of us. I needed someone to care for the children while I worked and she needed a place to live. The only good thing about moving into that basement was we wouldn't have to pay rent. However, we were stuck here for the winter. I could have entitled this book *A Winter of Hell*. I prayed we would all survive.

Chapter 19

Changes

In the fall of 1966, Keith was still working for the military. He'd been lucky enough to land the job and seemed happy there. He was a prankster and worked with a bunch of fun-loving guys who liked to drink, party, and play tricks on each other. Some of the tricks he played on unsuspecting fellow workers were hilarious, but could at times be very dangerous. We laughed a lot when we all got together. He enjoyed working there because all the guys liked his antics and his free-spirited nature. In reality, was he covering up for his deeply embedded insecurities?

Aside from that, he was feeling guilty about the whole situation he had put his family in. He kept busy working on the house. He did all he could to try and keep us warm. It was a good thing we had a dual-burning stove. We collected firewood from wherever we could get it to try and save on fuel. He worked extremely hard to make the basement liveable, but it was appalling, and it's a miracle we survived.

The first week of December after months of Keith not coming home, he came marching in the door, drunk again. I was beside myself with anger.

"Why do you do this to us?" I yelled.

"Cause you're a fucking slut!" he screamed.

Once again the fight was on. He banged me around a bit and left a few bruises, but I took it all in stride. I knew no other way.

The next day he was totally different and couldn't do enough for us. He played with the children when he got home from work. If he wasn't too drunk he loved to wrestle with them. He stocked up on firewood and topped up the oil tank using the money he would normally spend at the club. It would also allow a few dollars for Santa's visit at Christmas time. When Keith was sober, he showed me the caring and compassionate side of him that I loved from the first time we met. It was his saving grace.

One joyful thing our children liked was the hunt for a Christmas tree. Every year since we'd been married we had always gone into the forest and selected a tree to cut. It was that time again, so off we went. It was always the most enjoyable time of the holidays. It usually occurred after a fresh snowfall. The children loved to romp in the snow and make snow angels.

"Look, Mommy, see my angel?"

"See mine too, Mommy."

"I made the best one. See?"

We enjoyed traipsing through the new snow until we found just the perfect tree. After stuffing it into the trunk we headed back home. I felt reluctant to call that hole in the ground a home.

Keith never prepared the proper tree stand. He would put it in a bucket then tie it up into the corner with a piece a string. Unsightly to be sure, but that was it. I tried to cover the string with decorations, but could never find enough decorations to camouflage it.

Getting through Christmas was difficult. Sal and I scrambled around trying to find a few scraps of furniture, warm clothes for the kids, and anything else we might use to make their Christmas as normal as possible. We were delighted when Keith brought home a little table set and four chairs for the children. He had intended to give it to them for Christmas but we hadn't any place to store it so he decided to give it to them early. They were very happy with it! I managed to buy the children new pyjamas. It became a tradition of sorts. On Christmas Eve I would bathe them all in the big galvanized wash tub and put on their new pyjamas. We then hung woollen socks along the front of the television screen, as there seemed to be no other place to hang them. I lined the children up in front of our pitiful tree and took some pictures of them all smiling and cheerful. They were so innocent and as long as Mommy and Daddy were there, they were happy. My biggest worry was whether Keith would be home from the club before they went to bed.

That year, Christmas was an unforgettable experience in terms of amenities that an average Canadian family expects: access to fresh air, bathroom facilities, running water, and heat. We were extremely cramped for space as well, with my family of six and Sal's family, but we tried our best to not let the children suffer because of our living conditions. We were extremely happy for the little set Keith had given them earlier. At least they could sit and enjoy that little space for eating and playing with their toys. I was still working at the mess, therefore, Sal was a wonderful help while we were moving and was pretty much in charge of the house as well. She was very efficient with her left hand (our mother always teased her when we were growing up: Mom called her Left-Handed Paddy). Sal was very funny and made us laugh, at times when there was little to laugh about; her sense of humour, at times, took an intolerable situation and made it more tolerable. She lifted our spirits. I especially appreciated her for that. Even Keith was glad she was there.

Christmas morning was over quickly, and other than their table and chairs set, I can't recall what they got that year. I prepared the turkey for dinner, Labrador style, along with the infamous Jigs dinner, or boiled dinner as we'd called it in Cartwright.

The rest of the holiday season was stressful because it was too cold to allow the children to go outside. We were imprisoned in the basement.

Right after Christmas Keith and I went back to work. Keith went back to the motor pool. He was a heavy equipment operator and acting runway foreman. I went back to the mess hall. I continued to sneak food from the mess to help feed the children. Sal was such an excellent worker and was marvellous with my children. She knew my values when it came to the rules and knew how to implement them. They were formidable years, and my children turned out well, in a large part because of her. I will be forever grateful to her for that.

Early in 1967 there was talk that a lot of heavy equipment operators would be needed, as a massive Churchill Falls development project got under way, which our premier, Joey Smallwood, had been promising. There was also talk of a heavy equipment course becoming available to anyone wanting to take it. Keith saw it as an opportunity to upgrade his skills, to change his career, and to improve our lifestyle. However, he would have to go to Stephenville, Newfoundland, to training school.

"What? Stephenville! Where's dat?" I asked.

"Newfoundland. And I'll be gone for two months."

"Two months! What will we do in the meantime? We got no wood or water, not even enough money for fuel!"

"The government will pay me and I'll send money home."

I was still working so there would be one regular income. Therefore, after much discussion, I reluctantly agreed. It was hard to pass up an opportunity to acquire a better life for our family. After all, it was only for two months. Besides, I had a free babysitter with my sister, and with her help I felt confident I could make it through.

"When ya goin'?" I asked as we climbed into our pitiful bed.

"As soon as it starts, perhaps as soon as next week."

I was worried sick for the next week to think we would be alone in this strange situation without even a window to let the sunshine in or to see what the weather was like. Sal and I continued to try to make our home a little more liveable. The red and white tile-patterned linoleum brightened it up a bit. I can't recall where the furniture came from. I know we had a run-down couch and a couple of end tables. There was no plaster on the walls; paint was nowhere to be seen. We didn't have doors to any of the rooms. We did have a toilet but we didn't have a sink or tub. We had hoped to be in the upstairs by summer, but would that happen now that Keith was leaving?

A few days later he was getting ready to leave for Stephenville. I was very concerned but put on a brave face. It was hard to get Keith to talk about his feelings. It was even harder for me to express my feelings, but here we were, two very young parents of four small children, plus two other family members to care for, and the main breadwinner was about to walk out the door! What does one say?

"Take care of the kids," he said.

"We'll be all right. When will you send money?" I asked as he gave me a brief hug.

"I'll send it as soon as I can," he mumbled, and he was gone.

Chapter 20

Winter of Hell

In 1839, fur trader and explorer John McLean stumbled upon some mighty falls while trapping and named the river the Hamilton River after Sir Charles Hamilton, who was the Newfoundland governor at the time. He was awestruck at the magnificent sight in front of him. The mighty falls dropped 1,735 feet. In 1907, the development of the falls was brought up at a town meeting. In 1915, Wilfred Thibaudeau surveyed the huge plateau on the Hamilton River just above the falls. It was then suggested that the water could be diverted from the river before reaching the falls using the capacity of the Basin to cut out the need for gigantic dams. Thibaudeau's findings were validated by the Newfoundland Government in 1947. However, the resources were not available to go ahead with the plan to develop the falls. It was not until the British Newfoundland Development Corporation (BRINCO) decided to harvest the iron ore in western Labrador and a railway was constructed in 1954 to ship it to the outside world, that it became feasible to develop the falls.

During its development in the 1960s, the falls were renamed again. They were to become Churchill Falls. The early trappers travelled by foot up the great river from all points in Northern Labrador to hunt and trap for fur. It was known to them simply as the "height of land."

The powers-that-be got their heads together and made the decision to go ahead with the massive project. Brinco was to acquire the contract for the mineral and water rights for twenty years hence. The official name of the company became the Churchill Falls (Labrador) Corporation Limited. Established in 1961, they were granted a ninety-nine-year lease authorizing the company to develop Churchill Falls. It was to become the largest underground powerhouse in the world, and it remains the largest to this day. Churchill Falls had a force of 650 people to operate service and maintain the mighty falls.

An ad in *The Northern Reporter* called for men to work at the Churchill Falls hydro development project. Other than the iron ore mines in Wabush and Labrador City, this would be the largest development in Labrador's economy since the building of the military bases in the early 1940s. The whole town had been hearing of it for months. It was going to be gigantic.

Joey Smallwood, the premier of our province, came to Happy Valley–Goose Bay and held a huge meeting, which Keith attended. Joey promised that because there was a shortage of qualified operators, anyone interested in working in Churchill Falls would be offered a special heavy equipment training course in Stephenville, Newfoundland. This course was designed specifically to train men to work in Churchill Falls.

Therefore, Keith saw this as an opportunity to change the course of our lives. He had been working for the military as a civil service worker from the beginning: food services, supply, tech stores, and motor pool-heavy equipment parts and supplies. He'd never been out of work. He felt there was more he could do with his talents. When a training course was offered in Stephenville, Newfoundland, for a heavy equipment operator, Keith decided to take it. He could then apply for a well-paying job in Churchill Falls. He didn't tell me what his plans were. Moreover, because Sal was with me for the winter, and I wouldn't be alone, it would be a good time to take advantage of this scenario and train for a better paying job. I assured him that Sal and I could manage. So, off he went to

Stephenville for a twelve-week course in heavy equipment.

I started feeling ill shortly after he left for Stephenville, but I didn't want him to know, because he would worry and maybe not go. Plus, the promise of big money was hard to turn down. The basement was drafty and the children were coming down with colds. I hadn't talked to Keith for a week or so and there was very little money coming in. To make matters worse, when I phoned Stephenville, I couldn't find him. Finally, he called a few days later.

"Why didn't you send us money?" I sobbed.

"I gotta pay the rent and eat," he told me.

We had no choice but to struggle through the next several weeks. During this time I started feeling weak and sick. I thought it was the flu and stayed home from work for a few days to rest and get well. However, I didn't get well. I was feeling very weak and tired all the time.

When Keith came home from Stephenville I was never so glad to see him. He'd finished his course in half the allotted time and surprised me when he bounded in the door. I was grateful we had made it through his training course without incident. He proudly displayed his certificate.

"I'm so proud of you!" I beamed.

"Thank you," was all he said.

He never was good at accepting compliments. The children were so excited to see their dad and Keith marvelled in their joy. Except for my illness, our lives to some degree returned to normal. Keith started back to work. I tried to hide my weakness from him because he was a worrier and didn't handle things well.

In early March 1967, McNamara Construction, a company well known in the province for its ability to get major projects done, was hiring heavy equipment operators to plough and construct the road from Goose Bay to Churchill Falls. First a road had to be built. This is what Keith had been training for, to clear-cut the area in preparation for the road from Churchill Falls to Goose Bay. Goose Bay, with its excellent docking facilities, was chosen as the hub for shipping and receiving the supplies needed for the massive construction to follow.

Keith, with his heavy equipment operator's certificate in hand, went to McNamara Construction to apply for the job. The pay was excellent and he was hopeful that he would finally be able to provide for his family, finally improve their quality of life, and be proud of his accomplishment. After all, anything was better than the conditions under which we had been living for the past few months. He proudly submitted his application along with his certificate to McNamara.

The man behind the desk took one look at it and tossed it back at Keith. "We need people with experience. We're not hiring anybody just out of trade school," he barked. He went on to say "This doesn't tell me anything. That certificate doesn't prove you can do the job! Those instructors in Stephenville are no good and don't know what the fuck they're talking about." Keith was extremely disappointed as he left the building. Later that night at the club he overheard a couple guys from McNamara talking about the young punk that had applied for a job from *Joey's* training school in Stephenville.

"Maybe Joey would like to hear what you just said," Keith told them and walked away.

Keith had quit a civil service job with the government to take the course. Needless to say, he was furious!

Still fuming over what had just happened, and feeling helpless and powerless as to where to go next, Keith went about trying to find another job. After all, he had a large family to feed. He was hired by a local contractor as a heavy equipment operator on the Labrador Highway, or Freedom Road as it was locally known. However, it paid only a fraction of what he would have received in Churchill Falls. It was then he decided to write the letter to our premier. He never thought he would get a response, let alone a personal response from the premier himself.

He went to the local newspaper and demanded there be an investigation into the hiring practises of McNamara. He then sat down and compiled a letter and brought it to *The Northern Reporter*. The paper decided to print Keith's letter.

The Northern Reporter, Vol. 2, No.11, March 30, 1967

Dear Editor,
I have just returned from vocational training school in

Stevenville [*sic*], Newfoundland, after completing a five-week course as a heavy equipment operator. I have a certificate given to me by the vocational training school as proof of my completion of the course. As Happy Valley is my home, I naturally returned here with the understanding that jobs would be available on the new road being built from here to Churchill Falls. Upon my return I went to McNamara Construction Co. Limited to submit my application. I was informed there was no work for me, that my certificate, to quote a McNamara representative, "this doesn't tell me anything" was the reply given me. He informed me that the certificate didn't prove I could do the job, even though it was signed by my instructor and the principal of the vocational training school.

Now, I understand that the vocational schools were opened by the government to give the people an opportunity to learn a trade. I resigned my job in Goose Bay to take the training course. I successfully completed the course, returned with my certificate, and then had someone say, to quote, "those instructors are no good and don't know what they are talking about." This I disagree with because the course was an excellent one, and I would recommend it to anyone. I also know that McNamara is employing RCAF personnel on a part-time basis. Consequently, there must be jobs available. I suggest there be an investigation made in the chief personnel of this project to ensure they are doing a proper job and abiding by the conditions of their contract. Copies of this letter have been sent to MR. W.H. Rompke, President and Director of Labrador Affairs, McNamara Construction Co. Ltd., St. Johns, and, the office of the premier.

Yours Truly,
Keith Penny, Happy Valley, Labrador.

Because we were so overwrought with the bad news of recent events, I didn't want to burden Keith with my illness, and I struggled with feeling weak and sick from what I thought was a bad bout of the flu.

A week or so later the phone rang. It was a government official wanting to talk to Keith! The same day a telegram was hand-delivered to us. Shortly after that, an official-looking man in a nice suit came knocking on our door with a bunch of papers in his hand. They also looked official. They were from the premier of our province, Joey Smallwood! All of this was trying to ensure that Keith didn't cause any further damage. The government official had a letter, accompanied with plane tickets to Wabush, Labrador.

"No, I'm not goin'. I can't afford it, I got no money," Keith shouted to the man.

"You don't have to worry about that. It's all paid for," he was told.

What was Keith to do? He had no choice but to pack his suitcase and go. He was to fly out the next morning. He was told he would be briefed on the plane as to where he was going, why he was going, and what to do when he got there.

He knew I wasn't feeling well, but I assured him I was on the mend and would be back to work soon. Again, we were very grateful for my sister being with us. Needless to say, we had a sleepless night. What was happening? How did all this come about? Could it be because of the newspaper article and the letter to the premier? We didn't know, and nobody would tell us.

The next morning we packed Keith's meagre belongings.

"Will you be able to phone me?" I asked.

"I don't know. I don't even know where I'll be," he replied.

A horn blared outside and off he went in a taxi to the airport. He was gone! Where was he going? How long would he be gone? I was full of questions, in shock, and deeply concerned about what would happen to us now.

"Where's Daddy to, Mommy?" the children asked over and over.

"He had to leave home for a little while, but he'll be home soon," I assured them.

It was painful to see the uncertainty on their little faces. It broke my heart to think what they must be going through. I tried my best to get them settled so they wouldn't worry. They'd been keen enough to understand our worry and concerns. I had so many unanswered questions for myself as well. Where was he going? What would he do? How would he get paid and how much? How would he get the money to me? It was assumed he was going to work at Churchill Falls, but nobody knew for sure. There was no communication yet in Churchill Falls, there was no mail service or transportation, no roads, no phone to talk to him. We had no money, no firewood, and no means of getting it.

A few days after Keith left I became very sick. Sal called the nurse and shortly afterward she came to visit me. I felt so ashamed of our living conditions but she didn't say anything. I was instructed to pee in a chamber pot, and I was horrified to see that my urine was almost black! The nurse immediately took me to the hospital. I was placed in a room in total isolation.

What was wrong with me? No one would tell me. I was kept there for several days not seeing anybody! Finally I was told I had hepatitis; the highly contagious one. I spent two weeks in total isolation. Sal couldn't visit even if she wanted to. It was too cold and too far to drag five tiny children. So there I was, helpless, powerless, and shut off from my family. Could it get any worse?

Chapter 21

Hard Times

In the spring 1967 I had been away from my hometown of Cartwright and my family for seven years. I had telephoned my mother a few times using the old-fashioned radio system that required you to say "over" because in Cartwright there was no regular telephone system in place yet. They still used the RT set. Not only could I not talk to my family, there were no roads connecting communities in Labrador either. I missed my family terribly.

My father, Thomas Curl, was a quiet, mild-mannered man with a gentle spirit. He stood about five foot, seven inches tall with broad shoulders, a straight back, and a receding hairline. He was a polio survivor and walked with a limp. One of his legs was skin over bone, and when he walked his foot flew out as if spring loaded. However, it never slowed him down. When he married my mother, he gave her a .22 rifle and a sewing machine, a very wise move indeed. Both of those items were invaluable in keeping the family alive during his extended hunting and trapping trips into the forest. He played the accordion each evening and we would dance joyfully around the tiny cabin. I just wanted to help my dad at everything. I wanted to be with him! I loved to help and was proud of being a tomboy, even though I didn't know what a tomboy was at the time. But most times I was just "in the way" but he still called me by a special name: Jimmy. I adored him!

My mother, Florence Clark, was affectionately known to the locals as Aunt Flossie. She was short in stature but made up for it in tenacity and grit. She was in all aspects ruler of the roost. We could get a swift back-hander or a belt, a willow, or whatever was near her if we dared to disobey. Looking back I fully understand why she had to be strong. After all, she had to keep us alive while living in the wilderness. She'd made good use of the little gun and the sewing machine. I thank God for my mother, and even though she lost four babies in infancy, she raised ten of us to adulthood.

I'd just turned twenty-four years old in January of that year and had four small children under the age of five. My husband was away god-knows-where with no way to contact him. I was very ill and in the isolation section of the hospital all alone when a call came in. The nurse came to my ward and told me there was a call for me from Cartwright. She masked me up and I fearfully went to answer the phone.

"Hello?" I said.

"Is this Josie Penny?"

"Yes ma'am," I replied. I started shaking. She sounded official.

"This is Nurse Ann, from the Cartwright hospital. I want to inform you that your father passed away tonight."

I started screaming right there at the nurse's station. The nurse quickly poked a needle into me, which put me out immediately. I still don't know what they shot into me, but whatever it was I was allergic to it. I was out for two whole days, and when I came to, the nurses and doctors were standing at the foot of my bed.

"Welcome back, Josie. We were very worried you wouldn't wake up."

I was groggy. My mind wouldn't work. I was confused and somewhat baffled at all the people standing there, looking at me. It suddenly dawned on me what was happening, or what had just happened. I started crying uncontrollably again and the nurse gave me another shot. It was something else this time. When I woke up the following morning I was informed that my father had died of a brain hemorrhage. A few days later I found out the rest of the story. He'd been on a hunting trip with my fifteen-year-old brother Eddy. They each had a dog team. Eddy was leading and my father was following close behind. All was fine. Eddy looked back to check on him occasionally. A little later Eddy saw Dad leaning over and falling off the komatik. He rushed back to see him passing out. He decided to take him back to the hospital in Cartwright. It was the longest trip of his life, he later told us. Dad was rushed to emergency care but they were unable to revive him. He died later that evening in my mom's arms.

I felt so extremely helpless. I was heavily sedated and not in my right mind. The doctors were constantly at my bedside talking to me, trying desperately to keep me calm. I'm not sure if it was the drugs or the fragile state of my mind that caused the illusions I was having, but they were real to me. As I lay there with my eyes closed and in an altered state, I saw my mother as clear as day, weeping and grieving her husband. I kept saying to her, "It's alright, Mommy. I'll take care of you." I kept repeating to myself, *I know she's not here, I know I'm not dreaming, what's happening then?* I was acutely aware that when I opened my eyes, she would be gone. So I allowed myself to be with her and closed my eyes again. *Don't open your eyes,* I kept saying to myself. *Don't open your eyes.* When I finally opened my eyes, she was gone. I am not going to try and explain what it was. I don't have to. It was very soothing for my altered state. We cried together. I took comfort with the experience. My perception of what I saw in my mind's eye due to the drugs the nurse had given was so real, I can still recall exactly how my mother looked. I will never forget it.

Doctor Tsang took good care of me and spent as much time at my bedside talking to me as time would allow. It's a miracle that my mind stayed relatively intact, and I thank Doctor Tsang largely for that. Under the circumstances, with no one allowed to visit, no communication with my family, and no communication with Keith, I was totally alone. After that experience I will never underestimate the power of the mind.

It was springtime and the weather was getting warmer by the day. Finally, with strict orders of complete bed rest, I was well enough to go home. It was wonderful to see the children and my sister. I still hadn't any idea where Keith was or what he might be doing. He had no way of knowing about my illness, or he could even be dead! It took another few weeks to get strong enough to at least try to help my sister with the children, to gather firewood, and to try to get food on the table. There was none of either. How had she survived? What did they eat while I was sick? The cupboards were empty. The children seemed in good health. They were certainly happy that Mommy was home, and they looked like they suffered no ill effects. Sal was good to them. The way she ruled our household, though pitiful in its conditions and appearance, was orderly and under control.

The only money we had coming in was sick pay from my job. In the following days during a cold spell we were in dire need of firewood. We hadn't any money for fuel, so we had no choice but to go out after dark and rummage the neighbourhood for scraps of wood to keep us all from freezing. We stole from woodpiles and garbage bins. We stole from doorsteps and wood sheds. We did what we had to do to survive.

Mr. Carson was the manager of the Hudson's Bay store. I'd heard that under certain circumstances he would release food on credit. As much as I dreaded having to ask Mr. Carson for food, I had no choice. My children were hungry! I walked to the store in the freezing cold and my heart was pounding as I approached the manager's counter to tell my sad tale.

"Hello, Mr. Carson. Keith is gone to Churchill Falls and I have no way to reach him, an we got no food in de house for the children, an I've been in de hospital, an my Daddy died while I was in there an, an ..." I mumbled rather breathlessly; then I started to cry right there in the store.

"My, oh my," was all he could say. After a moment of trying to absorb what he'd just heard, he asked, "When did Keith leave and how long has he been gone?"

"Three weeks."

I imagine Mr. Carson didn't want to get too emotionally involved in my situation. Realizing that Keith was working and he would be able to pay it back, he simply said, "Alright, Mrs. Penny. We will allot you fifty dollars worth of food."

"Oh, thank you sir!" I cried. I couldn't hold back the tears. It had been more than I could bear. I paid no attention to the odd looks coming my way; I just felt grateful to be getting food for the children.

One day shortly after getting home from the hospital, Emcee came to visit. I was extremely happy to see her, but very ashamed that she would have to see how we were living. I tried explaining how it had been, and even though she was very understanding, she was somewhat puzzled as to how this mess came to be. We hugged and cried together.

Another day while I was recuperating my sister Rhoda came to visit me. She had been living common-law with Howie for several years and had a couple of children by then. We had kept in touch and visited back and forth during those years, but we never did become really close. I thought she might have had a drinking problem, but wasn't sure. In any case it was great to see her.

I was getting sicker and sicker, so Sal called the hospital and the nurse picked me up and carted me back to the hospital. I was informed that we would have to get out of this basement and find a decent place to live because it was deemed uninhabitable. When I returned from the hospital in April I was still extremely weak and was instructed to remain in bed at all times. Sal took good care of me and literally had to put her own life on hold to do so.

As soon as I was strong enough to get out, I started looking for a place to live. I was able to talk Dale Earnest into letting me rent a place on the corner of Grenfell Street and Grand Street in Happy Valley, and even though it was small, it had a couple of bedrooms and a useable bathroom. I felt rich! A real bathroom with running water and a toilet we could flush! Keith was still in Churchill Falls working. There was no way of letting him know anything that had been happening to his family. Sal and I went about preparing for the move. How would we do it? I was still weak and tired easily, so Sal did most of the packing, but we needed transportation. Who would I get to help us? I thought of Bruce, Keith's brother. I called him to ask if he would help. When he arrived I was very relieved. He'd had no idea of our living conditions, so he didn't know that there weren't any windows in the basement and that we had been living without natural light for almost four months. Consequently, when Bruce brought my one-year-old baby up from that basement into the bright spring sunshine, he was blinded and covered his eyes in pain.

"I'll never forget Mark's reaction," Bruce told us later.

There were several reasons for this dramatic reaction to the sunlight. In the past I had always prided myself in getting my children outside for fresh air and sunshine as often as possible. It was a given. Even when they were tiny babies I would bundle them up and set them outside to nap, unless it was too cold or too stormy. The dire circumstances leading up to this unfortunate time in my life — with my illness, being hospitalized for several weeks, the tragic death of my father, worrying about my mother, and especially whether my husband was dead or alive — left me temporarily insane and in no condition to worry about getting my

The Penny children sitting on a table in the basement of our unfinished house on Grenfell Street in 1967. Gregory was six, Mark one, Cathy three, and Darlene five.

children outside. The struggle during this horrific time was trying to survive, literally!

Sal, Rhoda, and I felt terribly guilty about not being there for our mother during her time of grief. There were three of her daughters in Happy Valley who couldn't get back to Cartwright for the funeral. Rhoda was stuck in a situation similar to mine, being involved with Howie and their children. Sal was stuck taking care of my family, and I was in the hospital. Therefore, the only family members available to help Mom were Marcie and our oldest brother Edward. Winnie, Dora, Phillip, and Linda were too little. Even though the whole community of Cartwright pulled together and rallied around grieving families, Mom still had five small children to care for: Eddy, Winnie, Dora, Phillip, and Linda. It would have been wonderful to have her three older daughters there in her time of great sorrow. When I thought about my mom, I tried to push the situation out of my mind. I couldn't imagine how she would raise the remaining six children on her own. I should have never underestimated her. She had many jobs. She was the community cleaning woman for the Royal Canadian Mounted Police's new house, the Anglican Church, the Marconi Station, the Hudson's Bay store, and the school. She did sewing for the Grenfell Mission craft store, and she also hooked beautiful mats. Some years later I was fortunate enough to be visiting my mother when she received her first old age pension check. She was overwhelmed.

"Dis is the most cash I've ever seen in me life!" she'd beamed, as she fanned it out in front of us. I took a picture of her holding her money.

Now, several weeks after my father's death, we were settling in our new residence. I was still not well, still didn't know where my husband was, and still had no way of contacting him.

Chapter 22

Keith's Hell

In April 1967, Keith came back from Churchill Falls. My heart went out to him as he told me of the terrible hardships he'd endured in the dead of winter while working in Churchill Falls. First of all, he was housed in a campsite with the engineers. Keith himself didn't know why he was there or where he was supposed to work. He sat around for the first two weeks being fed well and paid well but with nothing to do. Finally, he went to the project manager and asked them when he could start work. They didn't know why he was there either until Keith told them.

"Oh, you're Joey's boy," they said.

Keith was then assigned a machine and sent a long way into the bush. He was so far into the wilderness that he had to tow his shack containing food behind his snow machine.

"What did you eat?" I asked.

"They made sure I was well fed," he said. "I had T-bone steaks, pork chops, and all kinds of rich foods."

He told me of the many times he got caught in blinding snowstorms and couldn't see anything but a wall of snow. Then one night, after hours of driving his machine through the blizzard, he saw a dim light flickering far away into the forest.

"I was mesmerized and couldn't believe what I thought I'd seen," he told me later.

"Well? What was it?"

"As I got closer and closer I could see that it was an oil lamp in a tent."

He had been sleeping in his machine for so long that he started to become delusional and started to think he'd never return to humanity. He was overwhelmed and relieved to finally see human beings.

He put markers on his machine so that he would be able to find it in the morning and headed for the light. When he finally reached the source of light, it was a family of Natives. They couldn't speak English but motioned him to a sleeping spot on the floor of the tent. He literally passed out from exhaustion and when he woke up in the morning the Natives were gone.

When he returned to headquarters a few weeks later, his employer in Churchill Falls called him into the office. He was holding a telegram in his hand.

"Someone in your family — a brother, a sister, your father, or some-body — has died."

They then handed him a huge pile of letters that had been accumulating while he was in the bush. They hadn't bothered to inform him they'd arrived. When he found out they were from me, he quit. He became extremely distraught in not knowing who had died in his family. He grabbed the letters, stomped out of the building, and headed for the plane that had just landed. Eastern Provincial Airways landed a DC-3 on the makeshift runway every day to service the contractors and employees. He read the letters I'd written him on the plane on the way home. In those letters was the sad story of how sick I'd been and that it was my father who had died. He felt terribly guilty that I'd had no help or support during this very tragic time in my life.

"I will never work away from home again," he promised.

We were all so glad to see him back home with us. In the spring of 1967 Keith went to work for the Ministry of Transport as a heavy equipment operator. With the money he'd brought home, he decided to buy himself a car and put it in service as a taxi to make some extra money. I was very proud that we could afford something of value. I thought the taxi business was doing well. Then one day a huge tow truck arrived and a man started hooking it up to our car.

"What the hell do you think you're doin'?" I yelled.

"Taking your car, ma'am. It's been repossessed."

"What do you mean repossessed?" I screamed. "What do dat mean?"

"It means you didn't make the payments, so it's no longer yours."

As I watched the tow truck pull our first new car we'd ever owned out of the driveway I wept. What was going on with Keith? I didn't have any answers for anything, only questions. They kept piling up in my brain. Life seemed to be one tragic thing after another. I had no idea what he had been through in his lifetime. He didn't talk much about his childhood, and I didn't ask. I didn't even know where or how he had grown up.

With much prompting, Keith's sad story gradually came into focus. Mr. and Mrs. Penny were much older than most parents when Keith was born. His mother was forty-seven and his dad was fifty-six. Their youngest child, Graham, was nine years old when this beautiful blond-haired baby was forced into their lives. He was an unexpected child. Therefore, poor little Keith was not welcomed with great joy, and grew up feeling "always in the way." It felt like he was an only child as well. He became rebellious and angry at a young age. To make matters worse, his sister Mabel also had a son born one day after Keith, and they named him Keith as well. The two Keiths were forever being compared with each other. Keith Penny always ended up feeling less than his nephew and all his other cousins as well. His oldest brother, Jack, ran the family fishing enterprise in Battle Harbour, Labrador. One day Keith stole Jack's fishing boat and accidently ran it into a schooner. Jack was very upset with him. It caused a lot of damage and Keith was deemed a troublemaker and not to be trusted.

Another story in particular comes to mind: Jack was taking his mom to see a movie at the American Weather Station. Delighted, Keith hopped aboard the boat.

"No kids tonight," Jack said.

Keith watched as Jack left the wharf, then pulled in to a small island, just five hundred yards away, and picked up his own kids and went to the movie, leaving Keith staring in horror and hurt. Poor little Keith was devastated. He told me several times over the years of another incident where he wanted to go with his mom to a party. She smacked him so hard she put him through a glass door and split his head open. Then she just went off and left him.

Each summer when he got out of school, he was pawned off on one of his eight siblings, who, for the most part, didn't want him either. He was shipped to his sister Margaret's in Twillingate, Newfoundland, one year, then off to the lumber camps in Main Brook with Mabel the next summer, off to his brother George's in Elbow Cove the next year, to Adolph's in Deer Lake the next year, then to Mabel's in Corner Brook in 1956 and 1957. When he was seventeen, he went back to Adolph's in Glovertown. While at Adolph's that summer he decided to leave Newfoundland for good and headed for Goose Bay to look for work.

He started as a busboy and worked catering to the military personnel who were working on the runways servicing the aircraft maintenance men. It was there that Keith was introduced to beer for the first time. He was there for three years before his brother Graham moved to Happy Valley in 1960. Shortly afterward, Graham built a house for his parents, so Keith, who had been living in a barracks on base, then moved into the new house that was still under construction.

He was living there when I met him. It was just up the street and around the corner from where I lived with the Crawfords. We didn't realize until many, many years later that we were both very lost and had horrific abandonment issues. Keith was very quick-tempered and could be extremely violent when he was drinking. Why didn't I know any of this? We never talked about it. I found out one day in the summer of 1968 how angry he actually was and how out of control he could become. He'd had no sense of self, place, or belonging. Like me, he was a lost soul.

Chapter 23

A Terrible Accident

On July 8, 1967, Gregory turned six and I wanted to hold a birthday party for him outside. I acquired a sheet of plywood and I put it on the sandy ground and covered it with a white sheet. I picked up all the party hats, balloons, and everything needed from the local store and placed them neatly on the plywood sheet.

"I hope the wind don't come up," I said to Sal, as we put the finishing touches on the cake.

"If it does we'll just move 'em all inside," she said.

There were lots of children attending. Rhoda had a couple, Joan Clark from Cartwright had twin girls, the neighbour's children came, and Dale and Marge's children came as well. They owned the apartment we were renting. I was determined to give my children the best that our circumstances would allow. It was a nice little party. No one seemed to mind that it was on a piece of plywood sitting on the ground.

During the summer we were all suffering from the heat, so when we got an offer from a friend to go swimming in Goose River we jumped at the chance. I didn't know how to swim yet and was very watchful of the children going into the water. They were so happy to go paddling. I was satisfied, as long as they stayed close to shore. Shortly afterward somebody came running toward us shouting.

"A little boy just drowned right there where your kids are right now!"

"Oh no!" I screamed.

"Yes, didn't you hear the helicopter?"

I went into a panic. Yes, I'd heard the helicopter, but that was nothing new around here. I screamed at the children to come out of the water. They were not happy, but when I told them why, they obeyed. We were very disturbed that this had happened to a little boy, and decided to get out of there as soon as possible. I had heard many times that this was a dangerous river, but we were also informed the area of the river we were in was calm and safe enough for swimming. I became angry that there were no postings or warning signs.

On July 23, 1967, our oldest daughter, Darlene, turned five. I don't recall when it started, and for reasons I will never know, she was turning out to be a needy, clingy child. She wanted to follow me everywhere. In hindsight I had been preoccupied with all that had been happening with work, illness, the death of my father, and Keith being away. Then there was our appalling living conditions. It's a wonder I could function at all. We had a little birthday party for Darlene, but held it inside this time. She had the sweetest, doll-like features, with big blue eyes and thick brown hair. Something was off, but I couldn't figure it out. I simply didn't know that anything psychological might be wrong with her. I was puzzled when I would catch her rocking and banging her head against the back of the couch so hard she would rattle the front legs off the floor. I was at a loss as to what to do. Darlene was not examined or seen by a doctor for her behaviour. Were there tests available at the time? If so, I never knew and didn't have the insight to investigate. Maybe if she had been diagnosed and treated, our lives could have turned out much differently.

By late summer I was feeling stronger each day. I thought I might go back to work once I got the children settled in school. Sal decided to go back home to Cartwright. I would surely miss her and our children would miss their cousin Steven. He was such a sweet little boy and had become a special part of our family.

Halloween was coming soon and we always enjoyed dressing the children for trick-or-treating. Shortly after Halloween, we were getting ready to settle in for the winter. Things were almost normal in our family. We had been through a winter of hell and now we were all together again and starting to enjoy each other. Gregory was six, Darlene was five, Cathy was three, and Mark was just over a year. Mark kept stripping his clothes off and running around in the buff. It was a challenge to keep him dressed. *Where did I get such beautiful children?* I wondered as I prepared them for their baths. It was such a joy to have a bathtub with hot and cold running water.

A few weeks later I needed to run across the street to Pardy's store to pick up a last-minute ingredient to finish off my supper dish. I heard Darlene call, "Mommy, Mommy! I wanna come with you!"

I turned and in horror I saw that she was heading right into the street and into an on-coming taxi! Everything happened so quickly but seemed to be in slow motion at the same time.

"Darlene! *Stop, Stop, Stop!*" I screamed. But I was too late. It hit her.

I saw her tiny body hurled through the air like a rag doll and land about ten feet away. Horrified, I ran to her. She was lifeless and bleeding from her nose and ears. I picked her up and yelled to the taxi driver. Thank God he had stopped.

"Take me to the hospital. Take me quick!" I screamed.

It was only a few minutes to the hospital and I prayed all the way. Looking at her lifeless body bleeding from every opening in her head I kept saying, "Please God, don't let her die, don't let her die." Then she stopped breathing.

"Hurry, hurry!" I screamed to the driver. "She's not breathing! *Oh Dear God, please don't let my baby die!*" When we reached the hospital I ran inside. Somebody yanked her out of my arms. Dr. Tsang started wiping the blood from her face, which was now blue.

"Never mind wiping the blood away, just get her breathing!" I screamed.

Another doctor came and rushed her to emergency. Then, somebody rushed me out of the room and into the waiting area. I was all alone, pacing back and forth.

"Will somebody call my husband, please?" I managed to yell.

While I was waiting for Keith's arrival I was beside myself. The other doctor, Dr. Tooten, came out to say that she was breathing again but still unconscious.

"Will she live? How badly is she hurt?"

"She's a very sick little girl, Mrs. Penny. She has a fractured skull and a broken leg. But we won't worry about the broken leg until we find out the results of the damage to her head."

Keith came rushing in and we held each other and cried.

"What happened?" was all he could say. I tried to tell him but was too distraught, so the taxi driver tried to explain to him what had happened.

"Can we see her?" Keith asked the doctor.

"Yes, but don't be alarmed. We have her hooked up to life support. She's breathing and relatively stable for now."

As we entered the room, we were horrified. There were tubes everywhere and she looked so lifeless. We prayed and prayed. The doctor suggested we go home, as there was nothing else we could do right then. So we returned home. There were some friends there waiting who had heard the news, and we all prayed together. The terrible scene kept playing in my head. All I could see was her body flying through the air.

Around eleven o'clock that night, Dr. Tooten phoned to say that she had taken a turn for the worse and that we should get there as soon as possible. Images of her lifeless little body kept bombarding my brain. Horror stricken, we rushed to the hospital. When we got there the, crisis was over. Dr. Tooten informed us that he had called a couple of American military doctors to assist him, and was advised what to do to relieve the pressure on her brain.

"She's not out of danger yet, but she will have a very good chance of survival if we can keep the pressure on her brain in check."

"Oh, thank you, doctor, thank you," was all that we could say. We were given a little hope.

When we first entered the room, we were horrified once again to see her body hooked up to all those tubes. "She's a little fighter," Dr. Tooten said. "Can you call her name, Mrs. Penny? We need to find out if she can recognize your voice and whether or not she has brain damage."

Brain damage? I was in shock all over again. I couldn't think about brain damage. I just couldn't. I moved to her bedside, placed my hand on her little face, and spoke her name, softly at first.

"Darlene." No response. "Darlene." I spoke louder. "Mommy is here." No response. I put my head down closer to hers. "Darlene, Darlene, Mommy is here," I said, a little louder. There was still no response. I looked at Keith across the bed. One last time I put my face almost touching hers and yelled, "Darlene! Darlene! Darlene! Mommy and Daddy is here, baby!" Her little eyes popped open, her tiny hand came up to touch my face, and she started to cry.

"Mommy," she said.

She had recognized us! We were delighted, as were the doctors and nurses. There was a good possibility that she was not going to have permanent brain damage. The doctors still hadn't done anything with her broken leg. However, we were assured she would heal. They put a cast on her leg.

Several weeks later when the bandages came off we examined her little head. Her leg had healed but the left side of her head was completely flattened where the bumper of the car had dented in her skull. She was in the hospital for eight weeks, but she was a fighter and got to come home with us just before Christmas. Needless to say, it was a trying time for all of us. I didn't blame the driver. Darlene was out in the street before he realized what was happening. I knew there was no way he could have stopped in time. We were so grateful the taxi was there to rush us to the hospital.

It was a joyful Christmas that year. The whole family went into the forest to cut the tree down. I stood back and watched them playing in the snow and making snow angels, as tears of gratitude filled my eyes. Greg, Cathy, and Mark were happy to have their sister back. Their dad let them pull the tree to the car. Once home, Keith stuck it in the corner and, as usual, tied it with a piece of string. I, as usual, tried to hide the string with decorations. However, this time, I didn't fuss about it. I was just happy we were all together. Christmas was going to be good this year.

Chapter 24

Moving to Goose Bay

During the winter of 1968, following Darlene's accident, I tried to get on with my life, but nightmares and flashes of her tiny body flying through the air haunted me. I couldn't drive past that corner without moaning and hiding my face in my hands.

One day I gathered up the courage to tell Keith that he had to find us another place to live. I needed to get away from the accident scene, and hopefully get a fresh start. He was still drinking and coming home drunk, angry, and aggressive. It seemed I was fighting a losing battle with him, and not knowing anything different in my life other than abuse, I was becoming indifferent to it. When you have no way to fight, what do you do? What's another argument, getting hit so hard you're thrown to the floor, or slapped in the face? I was merely interested in finding a decent place to live, in the safety of my children, and in my own survival.

There had been several housing complexes built for the military and their families who would transfer in for a year or more during the war and post-war years. One was located just over the hill on what would later be named Hamilton Heights; one in Spruce Park, where some of the houses were built of wood and some from solid steel; and one on the Canadian base for the high-ranking officers.

Because of his job with the Department of Transport Keith qualified for their housing plan. In March of 1968 Keith came home from work with a piece of paper in his hand.

"What's that?" I asked.

"A house," he said, matter-of-factly.

"A house? What do ya mean a house?"

I started to weep for joy. We were finally getting a break. I was so happy! As it turned out, we were eligible for a nice home, fully furnished, with very low rent, which was automatically deducted from Keith's pay.

"It's a semi-detached Steelock in Spruce Park," he said.

"You mean we're gonna move to Spruce Park?"

"Yes."

Spruce Park was the housing complex en route to the Canadian base. The houses had high ceilings, three bedrooms, and plenty of room for our family. After all the stress and hard work of moving we quickly settled in. The girls took one bedroom and the boys took the second room. I then went about painting and decorating it to my liking. As I was painting the kitchen one day, I needed to get all the way up on a ten-foot ladder to paint the wall above the kitchen cupboards. I could feel that it was a little greasy. I slipped and fell to the floor ten feet down. There was nothing to break my fall and I landed on the solid tile-covered concrete floor. I'd knocked myself out. The next thing I recalled was the children bending over me, calling, "Mommy! Mommy! Wake up!" I assured them I was all right and continued on with my painting.

We spent the summer there. It had been a temporary place until a larger home became available. The size of one's family determined how much living space they could be assigned to. And because we were a family of six we were eligible for a house with a basement.

In the summer of 1968, Keith was still working as a civil service employee. He knew that better housing was available and applied for a bigger house for us, and we were fortunate enough to get one. We could be settled in well before school started and the kids could attend the local school without having to take the bus.

"Did you get us a place?" I asked Keith when he came home from work early one day.

"Yes."

"Where is it?" I dared ask.

"MacDonald Drive in the Department of Transport area."

"MacDonald Drive? That's a great area!"

I couldn't wait to see it! As Keith unlocked the door and we entered the house, I was overwhelmed and started to cry.

Our new home was located at B-33 MacDonald Drive, in the DOT area. The whole street was surrounded by a lush forest of spruce, birch, and fir trees. This DOT housing complex was built for all personnel responsible for air traffic control, an important job, to be sure. However, once the changeover began, the DOT then made the housing complexes available to all civil service workers; the airport grounds, roads, and parking lots.

The primary style of housing on MacDonald Drive was square, two-storey duplexes with flat roofs. They were very roomy and comfortable. I could not believe my luck. We had three bedrooms, a fully functional bathroom, a mud room, a big living room, and a kitchen with the most supplies I'd ever seen, and it was all fully furnished! I even liked the living room draperies. All we needed to bring with us were linens, clothing, and bathroom supplies. The children and I roamed through the house in awe. Was this really for us? Could we actually live like the other Canadians living on the base? The children each had a comfortable bed and a dresser to put their clothes in. Then when I went to the basement and saw the washing machine and dryer, I wept. This was too much. There was plenty of room for the children to play outside, as there were no gates or fences to restrict them. There was also a playground in the area and a park for the children to play. They were happy. What more could a young mother ask for? I liked that place and soon got to know new neighbours and made new friends.

Being civil service workers also qualified the whole family for a "pass," which permitted us to use the Canadian military's sporting facilities on

Christmas at B-33 MacDonald Drive, in the DOT area, Goose Bay, 1970. L-R: Cathy, Gregory, Mark, and Darlene.

base. I was ecstatic! I took full advantage of the situation and made good use of the recreation centres and sporting facilities. I enrolled in swimming classes that fall and went on to get my diploma to teach swimming. Not wanting to be left out, Keith also took a swimming course and got his teaching permit as well. I enjoyed it even more when I acquired the keys to the swimming pool and was able to take the children with me. They learned how to swim very quickly. By this time Gregory was seven, Darlene six, Cathy four, and Mark two. It was wonderful to see them as they frolicked in the swimming pool with their father. I thought I'd died and gone to heaven!

Going to school on the base was difficult for our children at first. I had to go about changing schools and getting mailing addresses changed and everything else that's required when one moves. My children were thrown into a whole new world. They were going to school with the military kids, and to the military kids our children didn't measure up. After all, the military children had been from all parts of the world and my children were born and raised in Happy Valley. I was worried that my children would be bullied and teased on the bus. Little did I know how bad it could get. They were made to feel inferior to the military kids and they suffered the consequences of those years. They were bullied and called terrible names. I was not as aware of this, although in other areas of our lives we did get much better. I appreciated that it didn't seem to affect their grades or marks at exam time. They did very well indeed.

We enjoyed the time we spent at B-33. The house was comfortable and I didn't have to buy furniture, which was the biggest blessing of all. There was lots of room in the basement, so Keith decided to build a boat for the children. Even though they were not familiar with boats or boating at this point in their lives, he wanted them to experience it as much as he did as a child growing up on the Labrador Coast. He got the idea from a boat he'd seen in a Batman comic book where there was a huge tail fin at the back of this bat machine. I was wondering what he was going to do with all the wood and thin sheets of plywood he kept toting down to the basement.

"I'm gonna build a boat," he said.

"A boat? In the basement?"

"Yes."

"What kind a boat, and how big is it gonna be?"

"You'll see," was all he said.

I didn't bother to ask any more questions. At least it kept him away from the club for a while.

It took him all winter and spring to build it. He then painted it fire-engine red. The question became whether or not we could get it up through the stairway. Well, we did, with less than an inch to spare! Leave it to Keith. It didn't resemble any boat I'd ever seen before, but it was pretty interesting to look at.

While he was working at the supply and truck maintenance shop, Keith was asked to demolish an old building. He came upon an old engine. It was an Iron Horse fire-engine pump. He thought it would make a great engine for his boat. He installed the engine into his "jet boat," as he called it, then took it to Otter Creek to test it out. All his buddies laughed at him and made fun of his invention.

"What is it?" they asked. "Where are you going to go with it?"

It made him feel awful, but there were lots of military guys who thought it was interesting and took lots of pictures of the jet boat as it sped across the creek, spewing up water from the back so high we couldn't see the boat. It was great, and it worked beautifully. However, Keith felt badly about the guys making fun, so he brought it back to the house and worked at it in the basement so no one could see what he was doing. It remained hidden away until we went camping a few years later. The name jet ski hadn't been used yet. To us, it was our jet boat. Were they even invented yet? Was Keith's the very first one? Did one of those guys who took the pictures steal his invention? We shall never know.

The first six years of our marriage had been difficult, to say the least. But I'm a survivor, and I was determined to make things better for my family. I was feeling well again, and strong enough to go back to work. I was fortunate enough to land a job with the Canadian Forces as a food service worker in the mess hall. I was hopeful for the first time in years that we could support our family and give them the things they needed. When I realized how much good food was being thrown away at the mess hall, I learned how to sneak food home. I convinced myself I was doing no wrong by taking it home to my children. Besides, other employees were doing the same thing.

In1968, lots of life-changing things started happening to our family. Keith's father died and we had to find money to allow him to fly to Corner Brook for the funeral. It was a sad time for him. When he was a small boy his dad held service and ran the church in Battle Harbour, Labrador, where Keith was expected to run the pump organ. He told me many stories that I would like to write someday.

When he returned from the funeral, Keith became very involved in the Squirrel Club on base. It had a kitchen with a small dining room used for the patrons and special events. Being a food service worker, I was elected to operate the kitchen and dining room. So now I was doing two jobs plus my swimming classes. I was extremely grateful for our live-in babysitter. I felt guilty that they didn't have their mother at home with them during their adolescent years. In hindsight, it must have been lonely for them. Plus, they were trying to adapt to a whole new lifestyle.

On a beautiful summer day in 1968, a knock came on our door at B-33 MacDonald Drive. It was the Royal Canadian Mounted Police looking for our seven-year-old son Gregory. Hank Shouse, who had started the first school bus service in Goose Bay several years earlier had put in a complaint. It was said that Gregory, along with several other boys, were blamed for breaking all the windows in a school bus. However, when the court case came up, the other boys' families had been transferred out of Goose Bay, leaving poor little Gregory to face the judge alone. He said he would never forget the terrifying experience as he stood before the judge that day.

"He looked like he was God way up there in the sky somewhere," Gregie cried.

We felt terrible for him. There was no debating the justice system. The judge talked to Gregory about the importance of not breaking other people's belongings, and what might happen to him if he did bad things. He was told not to break the law and about being a good boy. Keith offered to pay Hank for the damage, but he wouldn't accept any money.

Cathy was an adventurous child. She spent a lot of time outside exploring and playing with her friends. One day while roaming through the forest behind the house, they decided to start a fire. The next thing I knew, the fire trucks were racing down the street with sirens blazing. They quickly put the fire out. However, I did not know at the time who had started it. The consequence of this was a good scolding. Shortly afterward a decision was made by the DOT personnel to build a fire break around the whole complex. The final price we paid for this was that once again we were asked to move.

"Where we goin' to move to?" I asked Keith, when he came home with the news.

"I got us a house back in Spruce Park."

"We're going back to Spruce Park?" I queried.

"Ya, it's not a Steelock, it's a house, a single-family dwelling at 47 Park Drive."

"Okay, that sounds nice," I said.

And it was a nice home. It was close to Robert Leckie School, which was great for the kids. If I had a choice I always preferred the kids to not ride the bus to school. It seemed to be where they were teased and bullied.

I was getting tired of moving. Our final place on the Canadian side was 17 River Crescent in Spruce Park, which was also a single family dwelling. We remained there until Keith went to work for Labrador Airways in 1976 as a parts manager.

For the first time in years, I felt hopeful that we were going to be all right. Keith was busy with his job and also as the sports representative for the Squirrel Club, which unfortunately for the family, had become a major part of his life. Although he was still drinking and gambling, he did manage to bring home *some* money. Despite all of this, I was beginning to feel we could be a normal family.

Chapter 25

Entrepreneurs

In 1969, we were adjusting to our new house, new neighbours, and new surroundings. Keith was working for the Department of Transport on the Canadian side. His boss, Mr. Bob Howard, was a friend of Elmer from Moncton, New Brunswick. Elmer came to Labrador looking to expand his pizza franchise. He asked Bob if he would like to operate a pizza franchise in Goose Bay. Bob, in turn, asked Keith if he would like to partner with him. After much wrangling back and forth, the deal was set. The biggest attraction, and certainly for Keith, was that we didn't have to pay the franchise fee right away. We could pay it off in time from the pizza sales. Elmer would bear all the costs of setting up the shop. All we had to do was operate it. The decision was made that Bob and Keith would go ahead with the plan. Keith thought it was an excellent idea to make extra money. I didn't want to have anything to do with this. I didn't even know what a pizza was! Moreover, Keith hadn't talked to me about any of it. What was an entrepreneur? I'd never heard of it!

Goose Bay was filled with hundreds of American military people who were ardent pizza lovers, as were the Canadian Forces personnel, plus the hundreds of civilians who worked for the military bases. What could go wrong?

Elmer came back in a few weeks to set the whole thing up. They acquired a small building in the DOT area. We'd ordered the ovens from Moncton, New Brunswick. We then set up the huge mixer to make the dough. Elmer had ordered all the pizza pans, cutters, boxes, and containers. We were directed to the airport to pick up the cases and cases of ingredients needed to start our pizza shop. For easy access, Keith built the counter with eight holes to fit the tubs that held the ingredients, and he angled them at forty-five degrees. After installing the huge oven, he built a counter for cutting the pizzas on the opposite wall. We were ready to go.

Bob's wife decided to back out of the deal, so Bob had no choice but to back out too. That left Keith to tow the load himself, with very little help from me at first. Keith was determined to go ahead on his own, assuming I would join him. After discussing the possibilities of how successful the business could become, I reluctantly agreed. Thankfully, Elmer did the training. He showed me how to make the dough, how to place the toppings, how to layer them on the pie, how long to bake them, and how to cut them. He showed me where and how to get my supplies. I caught on quickly. Once it was done Elmer returned to Moncton. I was now the owner of a pizza franchise!

We had just become the very first pizza franchisees in Labrador. We needed a delivery vehicle, so we went to Labrador Motors in Happy Valley and purchased a Volkswagen. We then hired a driver to deliver the pizzas. We placed an ad in *The Northern Reporter*.

Once it appeared in the paper we became busy very quickly. In just a few weeks we were delivering pizza throughout the whole area of Goose Bay and Happy Valley.

I found it extremely difficult to ask for help and worked the shop myself for the first several months. However, I was wearing myself down and realized this was too much for me to handle on my own. So I hired a girl to work for me at night. People were hungry for fresh pizzas, especially the Canadian and American militaries. Therefore, we became a successful business. It was back-breaking work, especially when I had to pick up the one-hundred-pound tanks of propane from the Hudson's Bay store, fit them across the back seat of my Volkswagen, take them to the pizza shop, then drag them around the building and hook them up. They were heavier than my entire body weight! Nobody from the Hudson's Bay store would dig them out of the snow for me either. Nor did they offer to help me get them into the car.

My delivery boys were ambitious young men. Lloyd Hillier was a tall, strong young man. After working for me, he went on to start his own lumber and building supply business. It became very successful in the area. Another of my pizza delivery boys was Brian Tobin. After he finished school he went on to become a politician. He was very popular in the early years of his service for our province and later our country. He eventually became the premier of Newfoundland and Labrador! I was proud of that fact. "I gave Brian Tobin his first job," I'd brag to my friends when he became a popular politician. We also hired a guy named Tom as a driver. He did a good job for us as well.

I hired a young lady named Dorothy Noseworthy from Newfoundland as a nanny for our children. Dotty lived with us and took good care of our four growing children full time. They all liked her. I thought she did a marvellous job with them. After we hired staff for the pizza shop and a full time babysitter for the children, we were given the opportunity to live the high life for a while. Now that I was a proud owner/operator of Elmer's Pizza and working my butt off, Keith decided it was a good time to party. And party he did. He was still enjoying himself, gambling and spending all his paycheque, plus a lot of our pizza profits as well. I was beside myself with frustration and stress as I tried to carry the load on my own. He became very abusive when he drank, and would knock my body to the floor with one swipe of his big hand. Then he would beg for forgiveness afterward.

I was no angel either. I was lonely, frustrated, and eventually became a flirt. I craved and lapped up the attention bestowed on me from lonely men without partners and even a few with wives and families while inebriated at the night clubs. Oh God, I wish I could erase the flirtations and start all over with Keith.

When we started running into financial stress, I decided to lay off my delivery boys and deliver the pizzas myself. I would go to the Goose Hilton, the men's barracks, and barge in with their orders. It was the only high rise in all of Happy Valley–Goose Bay. Its six storeys stood out against the brilliant Labrador sky.

"Elmer's Pizza up!" I yelled as I opened the door.

Sometimes I would see men strutting around in their underwear and when I saw a guy walking the corridor bare buffed I felt very uncomfortable. I didn't know whether to keep going or run. However, I got used to it after a while and it didn't bother me. I was doing my job, plain and simple. Keith eventually found out.

"What the hell are you doin', goin' into the men's barracks by yourself?" he yelled.

"My job!" I yelled back. "You're not there, are you?"

"You're nothing but a whore."

"Oh ya? Well you're nothing but a drunken, no-good bum!" I screamed. And the fight, once again, was on.

A few years after we opened up the second pizza shop in Happy Valley and got it running smoothly. Keith decided we should also buy the chicken franchise that somebody had recommended for the area. After all, we were doing fairly well with Elmer's Pizza. So, we bought a Dixie Lee Chicken franchise.

I was not a good employer in terms of keeping track of my money and supplies. A handful of mushrooms, a handful of bacon, and a chunk of cheese became tempting to my employees and they began taking food home on regular basis. I went in to work one day and saw a neat little package sitting on the counter. Unfortunately for her, the girl had forgotten to take the package home the night before. I had to fire her. I was much too trusting. Up to that point I hadn't any reason not to trust. Then there was the case of the missing cash. I usually left the small change in the cash register overnight and didn't bother to count it out. After a while, I noticed some missing. This went on for a week or so. Eventually, all the cash went missing. I didn't call the police right away. Instead, Keith and I devised a plan. Just before leaving for the night we sprinkled a fine dusting of flour on the floor underneath the window. Sure enough, when we returned to the shop the following morning there were footprints! The robber simply opened the window, which was located inside the counter beside the cash register, emptied the cash, and left. How easy was that? We then called the RCMP and reported it. We didn't press charges against the boy, who lived nearby. The police gave him a warning and there was no more stealing of our cash. We decided it might be a good idea to lock up the place, and take all of the money home each night.

"You were always going around with a huge wad of money this thick," my girlfriend said, holding her finger and thumb several inches apart.

We were making enough money to live on, to pay several employees, pay for two new Volkswagens for delivery, plus run the company in good standing. But for reasons I can't quite recall, I needed fast cash one day, and my delivery man offered it to me. Unfortunately for me, I didn't pay it back quickly enough to his liking. He sued me for the three hundred dollars! I didn't know anything about the law, lawsuits, or the court systems. This ignorance led to an arrest warrant being issued for me. I ignored the warrant. The judge's orders had to be carried out. Therefore, when the police showed up at my door to arrest me, police we'd been friends with, I was shocked! In front of my children I was escorted from my home in handcuffs.

"I would have gone in your place," Keith told me later.

"I know you would have, babe," I said, sobbing.

I was driven to jail and put in a cell with two drunks. The policeman said I could have the top bunk, so I climbed up into it and cried the whole night through. What had just happened to me? "If I could just get my hands on the little punk, I'd choke him!" I sobbed. To make matters worse, because this happened Friday evening, I would have to stay in jail for the whole weekend. However, the powers-that-be let me out the following morning, *on my own recognisances*, whatever that meant. It was a hard, fast lesson learned. The arrest, I found out later, was not for owing three hundred dollars, it was for not obeying the court order to appear in court. Who knew?

During 1970, business had picked up quickly and remained steady at Elmer's Pizza. I was learning the operation and managing it quite well myself. We soon learned everyone seemed to love pizza, including our children. I felt invigorated with the whole operation until rumors started flying around town about the base closing. People chose to ignore the possibility of the Americans moving out. No one wanted to believe it. I was still teaching swimming, and becoming an independent entrepreneur in spite of everything else going on around me. I'd gotten my long hair cut several years after I got married, and was now going to the hair dresser's at least once a week. I was known to dress well. I recalled when I was twelve I'd ordered some clothes from the Eaton's catalogue. I'd become one of the better dressed girls to roam the roads in Cartwright, tucked in the arms of my GI.

My business and reputation grew in terms of my career and entrepreneurial spirit. We did the Elmer's Pizza snow sculpture that winter. And as usual there was fierce competition during all other sporting events.

Keith was still doing his carousing with the club and his buddies. I went to the bank one morning and there was a guy there depositing one of *my* cheques into *his* account. I asked him how he got it. "Keith lost it in a poker game last night," he said.

The Elmer's Pizza snow sculpture, 1974. Keith was the Squirrel Club representative, and he chose the theme of the snow sculptures for the Squirrel Club.

Early in the summer of 1971, I needed extra people to work in the pizza shop. My sister Winnie came from Cartwright to work for me. She needed extra money to pay for her upcoming wedding. She had planned on getting married in July. I hadn't spent much time getting to know my siblings when I lived at home as a young girl, and I thought it would be a great opportunity to get to know her better. Therefore, it was great to have her with me. A few weeks later our younger sister Dora came to Happy Valley to work in the pizza shop as well. She told me that Mom had kicked her out after she'd become pregnant. It was wonderful to have them in my life again. Needless to say, they were excellent workers. Understandably so, after all, we'd been raised by the same mother.

In July, I became overwhelmed when Mom and baby sister Linda came on the coastal boat for Winnie's wedding. Winnie was getting married in North West River, just thirty miles from Goose Bay. My sisters Sal, Rhoda, and Dora were also there for the wedding. She was marrying Lester Montague from North West River. He was from a well-known family with a phenomenal musical history. Once they all returned to their homes, I hired some local women to work for me.

So being an "entrepreneur" was a good thing in terms of learning about running a business. And because I didn't have a boss, I made free time to go swimming or golfing, and especially to direct the kids' music band, the Kool Kat Five. Unfortunately, my husband was not on board. I'd had no personal drive to do anything spectacular in terms of my career prior to the pizza franchise. Keith was the one who made all the decisions and started up Elmer's Pizza. I had no say, no voice of my own. I just obeyed. I'd been well trained.

Chapter 26

Clubs, Winter Carnivals, and Entertainment

G oose Bay airbase was a busy place during the early years of its construction and development. Once the time and place were decided upon, in early spring of 1941, no time was wasted to clear cut, level, and gravel the miles of runways needed to accommodate the hundreds of aircraft that would transport troops and supplies across the ocean from Europe. By November of 1941, just seven months later, there were 1,700 servicemen and 700 civilians working and operating in Goose Bay. At the time there was little time for fun, because of the amount of work involved to get the bases finished and ready for the threat of war and to guard the North American continent from any country that might want to harm it. However, once the bases were completed in the early fifties it became clear that entertainment facilities would be needed for the troops.

On the American side there was the Arcturus Theatre, where the latest movies were shown every night of the week. The United States servicemen had excellent sporting facilities for indoor sports. There was basketball, racquetball, hand ball, and ping-pong. For outdoor sports there were tennis courts and a golf course. There was a club for each rank. Most of them had slot machines.

While they were stationed on the Goose, the Canadian military shared their base with the Royal Air Force. They'd had a small unit since 1942. The RAF later opened their own entertainment facility and named it the Bulldog Club, named after their aircraft the Bulldog.

While they were stationed in Goose Bay, the Canadian Military had top-of-the-line facilities to keep the troops entertained. Like the Americans, they also had a theatre called the Astra. It was located next door to the airport restaurant and held the latest movies. It was the first real theatre I'd ever been in. They had their own shopping facility as well. There was a curling club and hockey arena. The recreation centre housed a swimming pool and a mezzanine floor for basketball, tennis, badminton, and floor hockey. There was also a baseball field on base. Each club housed a pool room and darts boards.

By the time we left Labrador in 1977, Goose Bay's famous Winter Carnival had been going on for forty-five years. It came about as a need to help the isolated military personnel and their families get through the long, cold winters. It was to become a highlight and a major part of our winters in Labrador. It was usually held in February. Excitement, anticipation, and fierce competition arose to peak levels, as rivals would do anything to win, and to be on top in all sports. This heightened state of mind, body, and spirit lasted ten days. All the clubs competed against each other for the Grand Trophy. Each club had their own colours. Our club, the Squirrel Club (the only civilian club), proudly wore our colours of red and grey. There were twenty sporting events, and whomever won the most events won the grand trophy.

There was an ice fishing contest, log sawing, snowshoeing, beer drinking, and spike driving. There was toboggan racing, ice hockey, floor hockey, and a Robin Hood and Little John on logs in the swimming pool contest. Our little swimming group had a synchronized swimming show, and there were swimming contests, broomball, basketball, badminton, curling, volleyball, and water basketball. There was also a darts contest, pool playing contest, and smuk racing, where several people from one team would tie their feet to a piece of two by four and compete against the other team. It was so much fun to watch.

The most intriguing of all the events was the snow sculpture contest. It was a big event. Keith, being a heavy equipment operator, was one of the guys responsible for blowing an adequate amount of snow into huge, densely snow-packed mountains. They could be as large as a three-storey building. He then had to assemble his carving crew and equipment, which consisted of axes, chainsaws, shovels, and knives. All the clubs participated in the snow sculptures. It would take several weeks to get the mountain of snow to where it was recognizable as a sculpture. It was exciting to go around to each club and try to figure out what they were making. Some beautiful pieces came out of their hard work, though it could get extremely dangerous working for hours in the cold or a blinding snowstorm. But Keith and his crew always got them finished and painted just in time for the judging, which was done on the first day of the carnival. However, the winner of the snow sculpture was not announced until the final night of the carnival during the banquet, as was the over-all winner as well. There were some fantastic sculptures. One year Keith and his team did a church. It was huge, big enough to

The Penny children on a polar bear snow sculpture during Goose Bay's annual Winter Carnival, 1971. The Squirrel Club was the only civilian club that participated in the carnivals.

walk inside where there was a pew and several rows of benches that one could sit on.

The carnival also had a Carnival Queen. I was elected twice. I honestly don't know how that happened or how I was chosen the first time around. However, I do recall some crude looks coming my way when I'd won for the second time. I received some rather cruel comments as well. If I'd had my time back I would not have entered. The rule was that there needed to be representatives from each club apply for Carnival Queen, but nobody else from our club wanted to enter.

I had been teaching a children's synchronized swimming course for several years, plus taking another synchronized class of my own, therefore I was in good shape, especially my legs. The carnival committee decided to choose the Carnival Queen by having a group of us women from both sides of the base show only our legs. The rules were to lie on the floor, raise your legs up onto a bench, and have the committee member photograph them. It was then decided that the best pair of legs would be the winner for that year. I won!

I got to work crocheting myself a red and grey striped vest and hat. The main responsibility for the Carnival Queen was to visit other clubs and cheer for my club with all the energy I had in my tiny body. I even learned to whistle really loud like the guys did. All in all, it was fun.

I'd never heard of the word "entertainment" before arriving in Goose Bay. When I was growing up in the wilds of Labrador during the 1940s entertainment centered on the home. We were blessed to have a father who played the button accordion. Once his dogs were fed and the wood was cut and brought in for the night, the wood shavings neatly stacked under the stove for lighting the fire in the morning, he played his accordion for us, and we all danced around the wooden floor. My dad also made us toys from whatever he could scrape up from the wilderness. Geographically, we were totally shut off from the outside world. There were no roads, no electricity, no radio, or any other way of communicating with people. In my mind we were the only people on the planet.

The entertainment in Goose Bay was a challenge. There were very strict guidelines related to carnival activities. These activities brought a lot of fun and enjoyment and whittled away the Labrador winters with more enthusiasm and excitement than there would otherwise have been.

I used to wonder why so many people carried what looked like walking canes around with them. I later found out they were full of alcohol. It played a large part in the jovial nature and competitiveness of the whole event.

My naturally competitive spirit was heighted by the annual Winter Carnivals and we enjoyed every aspect of it. But we also participated in several other sports as well. I played broom ball. I ended up in the penalty box more times than anyone else. Being always the smallest one I felt I needed to prove myself, to drive myself, at times beyond my capacity to do so.

In the summertime there was baseball. Keith was a good ball player. He also played in a dart league as well. There was fierce competition between Goose Bay, Labrador City, and Wabush during the annual tournament season held each spring.

If you were as a competitive person as I was and wanted to be active, then Goose Bay, Labrador, was the place to be.

Chapter 27

Visiting Home

In the early summer of 1971, I started feeling a strong pull to visit my hometown. So much had happened and I was missing the connection to my family, my semi-nomadic lifestyle, and my homeland. I'd missed the freedom of roaming the land wash and boggy pathways in my rubber boots and climbing the rocky hillsides in my sealskin moccasins. That lifestyle was gone forever, and because of my mother sending me out to work at the early age of eleven, I would never again feel that freedom. My free-spirited nature had been severed. Having spent so much time away from home, I'd had very little time to get to know my family. I'd lost my sense of home and sense of belonging. To visit my mother and siblings back in Cartwright at this time felt right, so I called my mother. By this time there was finally a regular telephone service to Labrador.

"Hello? Mom? This is Josie."

"Who? Don't shout so loud, I'm not deaf," she answered.

"It's Josie. I was planin' on coming home to visit you in July."

"That'll be good," she said. "Is you bringin' all the youngsters?"

"Yes, Mom. I'm looking forward to seeing you."

"Me too," she replied.

My mother was not one for intimate conversation. I was trying to read her tone. I hadn't had much of an opportunity to talk to her in the seven years since I angrily left her when I was fifteen. Therefore, bringing home our family of six was a challenge for her. Along with my seven siblings, it would indeed overcrowd the tiny shack my father had built her in 1953. How would she accept my family? She hadn't yet met my husband, let alone the children. I was getting anxious as the time approached for our departure.

So I was going to Cartwright, and even though they had no idea where they were going, the children were excited to be going on a trip. It was greatly anticipated and I had mixed emotions, primarily because I was fearful of what my mom would say. I was still a young bride and mother. The questions kept piling up in my head. Would she approve of my husband? How would she treat my children? Was she disappointed in me? Was she still angry with me for leaving home without her consent?

In the sixties, unless you had money to pay Labrador Airways for airfare there was only one other way to get across the Strait of Belle Isle to the coast of Labrador and Cartwright.

The *Kyle* ran aground in 1967 in Harbour Grace, Newfoundland. She was the last of the famous, yet aging Alphabet Fleet, so named because the names followed the alphabet. They were also called the splinter fleet, wooden ships built in Scotland in the 1890s. Newer ships, such as the *Burgeo, Baccalieu*, and the *Northern Ranger*, plus several other boats, went into service in the mid 1960s to service the Labrador coast.

Excitement piqued as the ship eased her way into the dock at Terrington Basin in Goose Bay. Seeing her huge bulk and hearing the clanging of her anchor chains brought back so many memories of when I was a child. The old steamer certainly had been the lifeline for the Labrador people, as she'd been the only connection to the outside world. We'd lived off the land for centuries. Therefore, when the first trip of the *Kyle* had pulled into the harbour, everybody participated in the unloading of supplies. She brought us long-awaited, store-bought food, store-bought boots, all manner of household needs, and other supplies required to survive. We were especially thrilled to see apples and candy.

Goose Bay had a well-maintained dock system built and operated by the military and very unlike the system I left behind in Cartwright in 1960. People would risk their lives to reach the *Kyle* as little motor boats of all sizes and descriptions would chug their way through the choppy sea to tie up to the ship's side. At great risk, all freight was lowered into the boats and motored to the fishing stages. It was extremely dangerous when one had to board her on windy days.

As we all boarded the coastal boat I became overwhelmed. We were on our way to Cartwright to visit my family. I don't recall much about the boat ride, other than fourteen hours of exhaustion from trying to keep four boisterous children from going over the side. By this time there was a docking facility in Cartwright, which was a relief. I didn't have to worry about the children falling off the rickety ladder into the sea.

There were few vehicles in Cartwright, and not much had changed since I left home. I was fearful of what Keith would think of Mom's little shack that Dad had built. We'd been so proud of it then. But Mom kept getting pregnant and we quickly ran out of space. *Space!* What space? There were only two rooms and a loft. When we were little there was no room for beds. We slept in bins on the floor of the loft with stuffed feather mattresses to cushion the hard wooden floors. As Marcie, Sal, Rhoda, and I crammed into that loft, we had to be careful of nails sticking down through the roof as we made our way to our bunks. Shortly afterward, my big brother, Samuel, and Dad built a piece onto the other end: a bedroom for Sam and a second porch with a veranda. Dad ordered grey brick siding from somewhere and covered the outside. To us it looked fancy, but in reality it looked shabby.

The children had no idea what to expect. Gregory was seven, Darlene six, Cathy four, and Mark was two. Their father, being a worrier, kept them close to him most of the time. The children watched with great interest as the old ship's whistle blasted its way around the point and into Cartwright harbour. We had to walk all the way down to the bottom of the harbour on the low road carrying our luggage. I wondered what the children must have thought as we entered that tiny shack. There had been several new homes built around the bottom of the harbour. We all crammed into the tiny room that used to be Sammy's. It was the room I'd taken over after he tragically drowned when I was thirteen.

One day I wanted to go for a row in dad's little punt. During high tide Keith and I hopped into the row boat and went for a ride. It was a beautiful day on the water. Keith didn't have rubber boots and while we were out the tide had fallen. Therefore, he couldn't get ashore without getting his feet wet. So I let him crawl onto my shoulders and I carried him to dry land! I'm less than five foot tall and weighed one hundred pounds. Keith was five ten and one hundred and sixty pounds, so it looked rather disproportionate when he climbed onto my shoulders. I was so proud of myself, and the strength I had for my small size. People still don't believe it when I tell them.

Another afternoon Keith took the children out in the little boat; they loved that. The only water they had access to in Goose Bay were the rivers. Here in Cartwright they enjoyed being around the land wash, and boats. They enjoyed the freedom of walking the roads and going to the store to buy candy whenever they wanted to.

It was wonderful to see my siblings. Everyone was grown up and some of them were already married. My mother was quite indifferent to our children. It seemed she didn't quite know what to do or say to them. At times it was rather awkward for all of us. Mom was never an affectionate person. She was practical and stern and needed things to be right with her world; she was a no-nonsense person.

In my selfish, self-centered world, it had never dawned on me that Mom might be overwhelmed by having a crowd of five strangers that she'd never seen before land on her doorstep. However, she did the best with what she had, and we all revelled in her home-cooked food. She made wonderful meals of fish and brews, fresh salmon, and cod cooked in all the ways I remembered as a child. Not to mention the wonderful homemade bread neatly sliced and piled high on a plate each mealtime. She made the most delicious upside down cakes I'd ever tasted. Needless to say, we put on a few pounds.

My sister Marcie and her husband, Austin, still lived in their house on a hill about a half a mile up the road. We reminisced about Lockwood

School and how she'd taken care of me. I loved her so. They had four sons, Terry, Jeffery, Brian, and Tony, and a beautiful daughter, Molly. Jeff was born with cerebral palsy and was badly disabled. I recall him crawling down that hill because he was unable to walk. Austin was very short and very funny. He used to get slightly inebriated when we would go to his place and he would have us in stitches laughing.

All too soon we had to go back to Goose Bay. Keith and I had to return to work. It was tiresome with all the children, but they were good and they were happy to return to their home as well. With sadness and so many mixed feelings about my hometown, my siblings, my parents, and my emotional attachment to them, I roamed the ship thinking how I really didn't know my own family. I'd never spent enough time with them as a child. I wondered if I would ever get to know them. I allowed the tears to flow while watching the houses disappear as the old ship *Petti Fort* clanged her way around the point.

Now to find my children.

Chapter 28

Broken

I was back to work and the children were happy, and things had been good for a while. Elmer's Pizza was running well; I trusted my employees to do a good job. Out of the blue I decided to call my mother in Cartwright and ask her to come to Goose Bay for a visit. She said she would come.

A few days later I was beside myself as the coastal steamer tied up at the dock. We collected my mother and headed to our house. I had it all cleaned up and in top shape with fresh flowers and doilies on the tables. She was impressed. I was thrilled and couldn't believe she was actually here. My mother was sitting in my house! She looked all around and inspected everything.

"This is nice," she said. I was ecstatic.

"Would you like to go to the restaurant for dinner, Mom?" I asked the following day. She had never been to a restaurant before. There was no restaurant in Cartwright.

"All right, maid," she replied. Not to be confused with bar maid or house maid, maid was a common name used for most women during casual conversations.

I decided we would all go to Jim Fintas's restaurant. It opened up in the early sixties across the corner from Saunders' Restaurant. He served great food. So I swabbed the kids' faces and we took off to the restaurant. I was so proud to be able to treat my mom with this brand new experience. We settled into a nice big booth and she looked all around. She seemed a tad overwhelmed and I was in awe of it all as well. She chatted with the children and tried telling them what I was like as a little girl. They were too young to contribute much, but it was all good. The menus came and I suddenly remembered that she hadn't much education. Would she be able to read the menu? Why hadn't I thought of it before? As it turned out she wanted to try the fish and chips. Jim made fantastic chips, so we ordered our food and waited patiently for it to arrive. Mom asked me how we were doing and where Keith was working.

"He works for the military," I told her. "He's a heavy equipment operator."

"Where's the pizza shop den?" she asked.

"It's up the road a ways, I'll show you later."

The waitress was coming across the floor with a huge tray of food when Keith, on his dinner break and wanting to know why his dinner wasn't ready, came barging through the door. He spotted us immediately. Then he rudely stopped the waitress in her tracks.

"Where you goin' with that?" he asked.

"I'm delivering food to this table," she replied, nodding her head toward our table and not knowing what to do.

"Oh no, you're not deliverin' it anywhere. You can take it right back to where the fuck you got it because they won't be eating it here!" he yelled.

I saw all the customers look on in horror. The poor girl had no choice but to head back to the kitchen with the food as Keith continued on to our table.

"And *you*," he shouted, pointing his finger in my face, "can get up outta that seat and get the fuck home where you belong!"

I was horrified! This couldn't be happening. But it was. I was too shocked to even respond.

"What the fuck do you think your doin', sittin' there like you own the place and me comin' home with nothing to eat? Now get up off your fuckin' arse and get home and get my dinner."

We had no choice but to get up and go. Walking out the door that day I could feel all the people glaring at us. It was the most humiliating and degrading experience of my entire life. I couldn't even look at my mother. I didn't know what to say.

Mom couldn't wait for the coastal steamer to arrive to get out of there. She called my husband Mr. Penny after that; she couldn't even call him Keith. It suffices to say, she never had much to say to him in the few times they managed to be together. When I went to Cartwright to visit, I went without him. I was dumfounded and became even more afraid of him than ever. It was a sad time and it drove a huge wedge between us.

I instinctively raised my children as best I knew how, on the principles I'd been taught in boarding school and from my parents. Moreover, I was always mindful of cruelty due to the incidents in my childhood. Consequently, without knowing it, my fear of rejection and abandonment was severe. I did some pretty crazy things to draw attention to myself. I carried that sad state of affairs into my life with my children. The one constant during those years was to work hard, to drive myself beyond reason.

Although I wasn't aware of it, I was a lost soul when I married Keith Penny. When I turned twenty-one and Keith introduced me to the club scene, I enjoyed going out on Saturday nights. Outside of my children, my love of music and dance was without question my greatest joy. The local bands that played familiar country songs gave me something to look forward to every week. I was happy for a little while. Keith didn't care to dance, so I spent a lot of time on the dance floor with friends and people I didn't know. I couldn't handle my alcohol very well and seemed to get drunk quickly. Suddenly I'd be too drunk to dance, so I would walk around the block to try and sober up. I would then dance until I literally, at times, fell to the floor. I also wondered why men always wanted to overstep their boundaries. More to the point, no one wanted to respect their marriage vows. Why did they always want to flirt with me? Why were they unfaithful to their wives? Was it only me? I didn't know at the time I lacked the life skills to control my behaviour. I'd lost the ability to cope with people who wanted to abuse me, sexually and otherwise. I'd been abused as a small child in Lockwood Boarding School. As a result, I had lost my sense of place, sense of belonging, and, most tragically, my sense of self. I felt inferior to all people. Therefore, I went along with a lot of the sexual advances presented, simply because I couldn't say "no." I never had sexual relations with other men, it was a matter of not being able to stop the sexual advances and in some cases harassment from certain so-called respectable members of the community in which I lived. I will not mention names, but they know who they are. I understand now why I couldn't say no.

Throughout much of my life I felt most people were better than me. This put me in a precarious place when I had to interact with other people. As a little girl, I was taken advantage of so many times I thought it was normal. When I did learn through conversation, gossip, and life in general that it was wrong, I really didn't have it in me to do much about it. Even though there was no actual intercourse, non-consensual sexual activities and sexual advances from men seemed to crop up at the most inappropriate times. I was harassed by co-workers, or followed home from the swimming pool, and flirted with on the steam line at the mess hall. I was at a loss as to what to do about it. Especially when we were at the clubs, and even on the dance floor. What do you do when you're dancing with someone and they shove their legs between yours? I lived in the guilt and shame of my behaviour and traded myself for other favours.

When I was nine, while attending Lockwood Boarding School in Cartwright, I was raped in the woodshed by several boys. I didn't have the strength to fight them. It damaged me and I felt powerless. I lost the ability to fight for myself. It seemed that whoever wanted to take advantage of me could do so. At the same time, after a few drinks at the club I was a flirt. I lavished attention.

Did Keith act like that? He certainly attracted attention from the women and would flirt openly with them. No wonder I was jealous! He must have suspected something, and being an overly possessive, insecure person himself, didn't handle this very well. In my own mind

I was not fully to blame. However, in his eyes I was. So we would have violent fights.

Then one day, for reasons I will never know, I fought back. I suddenly became that tenacious high-spirited little girl from long ago that would take no crap. I was fighting for my children! I was fighting for my life!

It happened on Christmas Eve. I always expected and insisted Keith be home for the children on Christmas Eve. I'd expressed to him that he *had* to be home no matter what, that was the rule. Well, he didn't come home for dinner and he still wasn't home when it was time to hang their stockings. It was now past the children's bedtime.

"Where's Daddy to, Mommy?" they kept asking.

"He'll be here in a few minutes," I assured them.

"When we gonna hang up our stockings?"

The questions in their eyes were excruciating, and as the minutes ticked by I became consumed with rage. When he finally stumbled in the door, he was drunk. I guess I'd built up a good shot of adrenaline because I flew into him with everything I had inside me. The next thing I knew we were like two wild animals wrestling on the dining room floor. He couldn't hold me back. I punched and kicked with all my might. All Keith could do at this point was to try and protect himself from my insanity.

"Josie! Stop! Stop!" he begged.

I *couldn't* stop. I'd had enough.

Suddenly, out of the corner of my eye I saw them. My precious little children, standing on the stairs in new their Christmas pyjamas, watching their parents in the worst possible situation. I stopped dead in my tracks, placed my head in my hands, and wept. For the sake of the children I tried to pull myself together and calm down. I had to, because by this time, they were also crying and horrified at what they had just witnessed, and I was horrified for them. Keith had sobered up from the battle and didn't know what to say or do.

We all tried to collect our sanity and get on with the business of getting the Christmas tree tied into the corner with a piece of line, and we hung the few decorations on it, more in the line of duty than Christmas cheer. We had all been waiting for their father to come for so long; the spirit of the evening had vanished.

Another incident of madness happened one night when he came home after a ball game. I lost it — again. I was very angry at him, first of all for being so late, and for being loaded drunk. When he finally arrived home, he passed out without allowing me to vent my frustrations. So, I whacked him in the head with a piece of two by four. I'd literally taken my life in my hands, but I was so mad I didn't care! He had a huge black eye. His cronies knew it hadn't happened on the ball field. Suffice it to say, he had a hard time explaining this one.

I knew I was broken, but I didn't know how it happened. Then while listening to the radio, I heard a very qualified speaker on a CBC program use a word I had never heard before. She talked about the *depersonalization* of people in our world. My ears perked up immediately. She went on to explain that it involved people who spent long periods of time in jails, convents, and institutions where rights and freedoms were severely restricted. It sounded just like my time at Lockwood Boarding School, in Cartwright. *Did that explain what happened to me?* I wondered. My freedoms had been restricted. I was certainly isolated. I had no voice. Even though there were no locks on our doors, there had been nowhere to go and no one to confide in, no one to turn to or to hug me and say, "It will be all right, Josie." Even though I only spent two years in that situation, as a small girl it seemed like an eternity. For the most part because I was kept there all summer, while all the other children went home to their parents and I was left all alone in the dormitory, because of how I was treated, and how I was teased and abused. I went from a free-spirited, tenacious, happy little girl, to a nobody. That's what caused me to be very broken. My inquisitive nature, my sense of adventure was gone. I was torn apart from the inside. Because my innocence was stolen from me at such a young age I had become, without realizing it, a depersonalized person.

Chapter 29

Pets

Pets were a very important part of our lives. In 1962, our first dog, named Tammy, was a Labrador retriever. She was jet black, her coat so shiny it reflected iridescent blue. The children could do anything with her; she was a wonderful addition to our family in their primary years. There was no veterinarian in Happy Valley in those early years, so when she developed distemper there was nothing we could do. She died at seven years.

Shortly afterward we got a weird dog named Fifi. She was part Dachshund and something else. She had a long body, low to the ground like a Dachshund, but had longer hair. She was cute as could be. We also had a cat that kept having kittens and we didn't know what to do with them all. The children loved animals and our youngest son, Mark, was always dragging home toads and insects or a baby bird or whatever he happened to find in the forest behind our house.

Ivan and Heidi Tarsier came from Germany and opened a pet store in Happy Valley. I bought a small fish tank and thoroughly enjoyed watching the fish when I got home from work at night. The ease with which they swam through the tank soothed my soul. It quickly grew into an obsession, and the next thing I knew I had two fifty-gallon fish tanks sitting on a huge hutch in the dining room. I bought all types of tropical fish. During that time, someone was leaving Goose Bay and needed to dispose of their foot-long Albino catfish, so I took it. It needed a lot of room, so I gave it its own tank. However, for some reason it didn't want to stay in it! I'd come home from work at night and my Albino catfish would be missing. Or I'd come downstairs in the morning and have to hunt the house for my fish! I was informed that catfish could live a long time out of the water, but how long? It was rather amusing. One day I started smelling something terrible. It took a few days, but during my search I opened up a drawer and there was my huge catfish rotting in my linen drawer. When I started running the kitchen and dining room at the Squirrel Club, I moved the fish tanks up there. My customers enjoyed watching the fish while waiting for their food.

One summer we had a dog, a cat, three kittens, two large fish tanks, a couple of toads, and a baby alligator from the local pet store. In the summer of 1969 we acquired the cutest dog I had ever seen. The way we got it is, in itself, an interesting tale. My niece Molly from Cartwright was a student in school there and the teacher was from Florida. The teacher grew to love Molly and felt sorry for her because of Molly's living conditions at home. She was a beautiful eleven-year-old with straight black hair and big brown eyes. When school finished in June the teacher decided to take Molly to Florida with her for the summer. I was happy for my niece that she could get this trip and see a little of the outside world. On their way through they stayed overnight with us to await the flight, which left the following day. When they arrived, Molly's teacher had the cutest little Shetland Sheepdog with her that any of us had ever seen. We enjoyed a pleasant evening together. Before they left the following morning I casually said to her, "I'd love to own a dog like that."

"If there is one available when I get back I'll send you one," she replied.

As they left for the airport, she once again assured me that she would try her best to get me a puppy. As they boarded the plane I thought, "It'll never happen, I could never be so lucky."

A few weeks went by and I never gave the puppy a second thought. Then the phone rang and it was Molly's teacher from Florida.

"Would you like to hear your puppy?" she asked.

I was ecstatic! I couldn't believe what I was hearing.

"Yes! Do you really have one?"

The next thing I heard was a tiny whimpering of a puppy over the phone.

A couple of weeks later, Molly returned from Florida with my puppy in a basket. He was a tri-colour Sheltie and had all the features of a pure-bred Shetland Sheepdog. I was in love. The joy he brought to our family can never be measured. I slept on the kitchen floor with him for the first week. Now the question was, what would we call him? It was quite the challenge to find a suitable name for such an adorable creature.

Keith was lying on the couch and suddenly yelled "Pollution!"

"What? What are you talking about now?"

"Pollution. We'll call him Pollution."

It took some getting used to and everyone thought it was cute and different and original, except for our kids. The kids were not happy when they had to go looking for him at night. They roamed around the neighbourhood hollering at the top of their lungs.

"*Po-llu-uuu-tion*, come here boy!"

He was an extremely smart dog and it took very little time to train him. He even learned how to play hide and seek, and became very good at it. The children in the neighbourhood would gather around and Pollution would know what was about to happen.

"Wanna play hide and seek?"

He would come and sit next to me. I would cover his eyes with my hands. The kids would scurry and hide. Once they were hidden, I would say, "Go find 'em boy," and he would race off to find them. Once he found one he would bark and then race off to find the next one and bark. He did that until all the kids were found. Then he would run back to me, sit, and I would again cover his eyes and he would listen intently for where they were going. Once I removed my hand he would again run off to find them all. He just loved that game.

I enjoyed him and so did the children. I would take him for long walks and it was tiring because he never seemed to run out of energy. He gave me so much joy, but it was a slightly different story for the children. If he wandered off the property, then of course it was the children's responsibility to go find him. They didn't want to have to go find him because of his name. They kept telling me how embarrassing it was for them to be yelling his name out in the street. I had my pizza shop a few streets away and if Pollution thought I was away too long he would go to the pizza parlour to find me, or he would wait at the door until we found him. He lived to be eleven. I missed him so. He was our last dog.

Chapter 30

A Growing Family

During the sixties Happy Valley experienced many changes. Private enterprises and businesses started cropping up in Happy Valley and many areas along Hamilton River Road. For the most part, all our needs were met in terms of goods and services. Was there price gouging? I would imagine so, after all, up to this point there was only one of each business in existence, and without competition it would be very tempting indeed to not take advantage of that.

Karl Gruber, along with his right hand man, Martin, operated Labrador Motors. It was the only place to buy a car or to have your vehicles taken care of. Otherwise you had to go to Newfoundland Island or elsewhere to buy automobiles.

There were new speciality stores opening up all around us. Bert and Charlie Warr opened the first drug store in the early sixties. A young couple from Europe, Alvin and Heidi, became one of the first entrepreneurs in the Valley. They opened a sporting goods store. Dave Hunt opened a furniture store. We had two restaurants: Jim Fintas owned one restaurant and Frank and Doris Saunders owned the other. Household Finance opened a branch just down the road from where we lived on Grand Street in the Valley. We bought a furnace with the money we borrowed from them. A new vocational school was built just past the town line as you left the Valley. The Americans donated one of their jet fighters to the town and it was mounted near the new vocational training school in Happy Valley. A new civilian club called the Twilight Club was built in the same area.

One night while at the Twilight Club with my sister-in-law Margaret and her husband, I was dancing with a guy, and Keith, after having a few beers, did not approve. He started arguing with the guy and Keith grabbed him by his tie, swung him around, and pulled it so tight he lifted the poor guy off the floor and almost choked him. The guy fell onto the table, knocking it off its one leg and it flipped up and across my nose, almost knocking me out. I was bleeding and had black eyes for a few weeks afterward.

New companies started along the three-mile stretch of road between the intersection leading to the American side and the Canadian base. We finally had some competition for the Hudson's Bay store when a mini mall was opened in the Hamilton Heights area in the mid-sixties.

Our first newspaper, *The Northern Reporter*, was started by Herb Brett and his wife. A new post office was built in the DOT area between the junction and Spruce Park that serviced all the civilians living in Goose Bay. Charles Sheppard opened a dry cleaning facility in a small building near the Canadian side, and I worked there for a short period. Bert the barber was kept very busy in his shop just off the Canadian base. The Hudson's Bay was given further competition when a co-op store opened in the Spruce Park area.

Having trained for a heavy equipment operator's license, my husband was one of several men who cleared the grounds for a nine-hole golf course. There were no rocks to battle with, which made the land clearing much easier. The Ammaruk Golf and Country Club was in operation within a few months. Keith became a pioneer member. Our oldest son Gregory made the first hole-in-one there!

All the roads were now paved and well maintained. Every fall small trees were placed on each side of the road to aid snow clearing. Melvin

Woodward was another prominent member of Happy Valley. For many years he owned and operated the only fuel oil business, Woodward Oil Ltd. He later expanded all across the province of Newfoundland and Labrador. He then created Marine Atlantic, which operated the ferry service across the Strait of Belle Isle. Unless one had the money to fly out on Labrador Airways, it was our only connection to the outside world. Mr. Woodward still operates today. I taught his boys to swim.

The first new housing complex was built in Happy Valley for Labrador Linerboard Corporation. The homes were built for the men hired to harvest Labrador's rich forest. One would be impressed with the speed and efficiency by which the clearing of the land took place to accommodate the building of that housing complex during the 1960s. The timber was to feed the new pulp and paper mill in Stephenville. However, even though there was plenty of high quality timber in Labrador, the short shipping season, plus the cost of shipping the wood to the mill proved to be too costly and it was forced to shut down in 1976, throwing hundreds of people out of work. This new housing area was eventually occupied by people with other jobs in the area. It's still referred to as the Linerboard housing area.

A few years later there was talk of ski slopes to be built on a parcel of hilly land adjacent to the road to North West River. Thanks to Hank Shouse's ingenuity, we soon would be able to ski. Hank Shouse was raised in South Dakota and moved to Labrador as a young man after reading the book *The Lure of the Labrador Wild*. My first personal experience with Mr. Shouse was when he and his new bride Bella arrived in Cartwright in 1952 to run Lockwood Boarding School. I will always remember when they entered the dining room to introduce themselves to the children. I recall him being very tall and straight. Hank, along with the help of his friends, erected a ski lift at Goose Bay, and Snow Goose Mountain was created. I was delighted with this and purchased a family membership for fifty dollars. The children were thrilled when I bought ski equipment and new skiing outfits for them. They loved to ski. I will never forget how quickly they raced down the slopes. Mark, at age six, skied down the slopes without poles.

Alvin and Heidi Tessier opened up a sporting goods store in Happy Valley. It was in that store on April 20th that Keith bought Gregory his first guitar. He was ten at the time. The odd thing about this is it was his little sister's birthday. Cathy turned seven years old. She was a beautiful little girl with an infectious smile. She was the cutest seven-year-old any parent could want. Some of her little friends came over for her birthday party, including her best friend Wendy, and a few from the neighbourhood.

"I'll never forget my seventh birthday," she said.

"Why is that?" her dad asked.

"When I saw you bound up the walkway with a big box and a small bag I thought it was all for me."

When he came in he gave Cathy the small bag that contained a stuffed toy and gave the big box to her brother Greg. What was he thinking? Giving her older brother a guitar on *her* birthday? It did something to her free-spirited nature and she carried the disappointment with her for several years to come. She spent most of her time outside and often wouldn't come home for her meals.

A new magazine called *Them Days* was started and operated by my friend and cousin Doris Saunders. She received an honorary doctorate degree and the Order of Canada for her work. Using a little cassette recorder/player, she went about recording stories from the local seniors and started a quarterly magazine. It was a little book compiled of people's lives in by-gone days and focused on the harsh living conditions of the Labrador hunters and trappers and their struggles for survival. It grew to include the whole Labrador coast. It's still in print today; I have most of the volumes in my library.

Once the strict controls of the American military were lifted, Goose Bay became one of the best places in Canada to live. The cost of living was reasonable and the pay was good for the work one had to do. Membership at the new golf club for my family was fifty dollars per season, and membership at the ski club was the same. I didn't pay for the children to swim because I had the keys to the pool. It was one of the privileges of being an instructor and volunteer lifeguard. There is not one sport I can think of that we didn't have access to. The Winter Carnival was all-consuming. Therefore, winter in Goose Bay may have been cold, but we didn't notice. The children, though not involved in team sports such as curling, hockey, or baseball, were more into the individual sports such as swimming, golfing, and skiing. They excelled in all of them and had a lot of fun during the early to mid-seventies. Happy Valley–Goose Bay became incorporated in 1971.

Chapter 31

Camping Trips

In the summer of 1972, Keith was still working for the military and my pizza shop and chicken franchises were doing well. Keith might have made a conscious decision at this point in his life to spend more time with his family. Whatever the reason, he came home one day with a plan. We would take the kids on a camping trip to North West River. The children didn't seem to know what to make of this, this was so new. I'd never heard of people going camping around Goose Bay. It did sound like it might be fun. But were the kids excited? I don't recall a lot of jumping up and down for joy. Keith and I set off to the new sporting goods store to purchase tents, camping gear, and supplies. We packed everything in our car and headed for North West River. We chose a campsite about a mile out on a point, on the Native side of the river as opposed to the community of North West River.

As we were setting up I was concerned about the heavy cloud cover and the threat of rain. This would not be fun. Once we were set up, I went about preparing supper while Keith gave the children a few lessons on survival in the wild. He taught them how to shoot a rifle and devised a plan for keeping safe. Shortly afterward the rain started, and it kept raining for the next two days. On the third day, while it was still coming down in buckets, we decided we'd had enough. So we packed up and went home. Even though Keith was a good cartoon artist, it wasn't enough to keep them occupied for a week.

The following summer, 1973, we decided to try this camping thing again. This time we decided to go to Mud Lake, a tiny community accessible only by boat just a few miles up Hamilton River. We'd heard it was a beautiful place. Keith had purchased an old boat from somebody and painted it with red and white vertical stripes. Then we decided to investigate the site. It seemed to take a long time to reach the camping grounds beyond the village. When we arrived we found it was already occupied by a group of Innu, so we decided not to camp there. I was disappointed because it sure was a fantastic spot.

We picked up the children and camping gear, then went directly to Willow Island: a wee island in the middle of Hamilton River, with trees in the centre and a huge sandy beach all around it. We had so much gear that it took five trips in the tiny boat to get everything from the boat to our site. However, with everyone doing their share we finally got everything unloaded. We were all hungry by this time so the first thing was to get the food tent up to prepare supper. The clouds were building and it looked like it might rain so we got to work erecting the two tents: one for the children and a huge two-room tent for Keith and me. We had to hurry and put everything in the tent and try to get the other one up before the downpour. It didn't rain after all.

I had prepared well for this trip by preserving different foods in mason jars: pork, steak, hamburger, stew, salmon, trout, cod fish, and vegetables. I chose a jar of steak to celebrate this first meal. After eating, the children wanted to go swimming in the river. There had been some concerns from our friends of a strong current in parts of that river. Where we were there was no threat, but to be absolutely sure, we'd saved up enough bleach bottles to rope off a swimming area for the children. They were given strict instructions never to go beyond it. Moreover, while they were swimming there was always one of us on lifeguard duty.

They were happy as could be, as long as they could go swimming. While Keith watched them I went about preparing the campsite: setting up a kitchen area and cooking facilities and the beds. Keith dug a big hole in the ground to use as a refrigerator. It kept our drinks and beer cold as the sun pounded down onto the beach. It doesn't get dark in Labrador until ten-thirty, but I raised our children with strict bedtime rules. Even though I allowed them to stay up a little longer while we were there, they still had to go when I said it was time to go, even though it took longer for them to finally sleep. I was pooped, but content that we were going to have a great holiday. It was such a beautiful evening.

The following day Keith went back to fetch the jet ski from Otter Creek, where it had been stored for over a year. One of his friends, Dave Wheaton, and his wife helped us put it on Dave's truck. Once we got it to the river, Keith drove it to our campsite and simply pulled it up onto the beach. It was ideal for this area on the shallow side of the island, because it required very little water to float. Our friends were very impressed with this machine. It went fast and smooth. Keith pushed it to the limit, causing it to spew mountains of water behind it as the jet engine revved up. We enjoyed the boat's performance. It held our whole family, but, for safety's sake, only a few at a time were allowed to ride on it. I was proud of Keith's ingenuity and it was lots of fun. We revelled in the beautiful sunset, and finally parked the jet ski for the night.

The next day we awakened to brilliant morning sunshine, with the all-familiar Labrador chill in the air. I started breakfast only to discover the stove was out of fuel, and the fuel was left at home across the river. No problem; Keith made a fire outside to cook breakfast. The bacon and eggs were delicious. The kids wanted to go swimming right away, but I wanted them to wait until it warmed up a bit. So we went about cleaning out the tents while Keith went across the river for the fuel. While he was gone the wind came up. It didn't stop the kids from swimming and we spent all morning in the river. When we got back to the tent everything was covered in sand! Keith had to cut a big log to secure the tent, as it had shaken loose with the wind. I prepared sirloin steak, potatoes, and corn for lunch. It was delicious. The boys did the dishes while I took a nap. The wind had died down and Keith took the kids swimming again.

Our family on the jet boat Keith built, circa 1973.

I woke up to company. My brother-in-law Bruce and his wife Dorcass dropped by for a visit with their son Larry. They were impressed with our setup, and even more so when Keith pulled a nice cold beer from the underground fridge. We watched the kids swimming. They lined up on their foam float boards and Larry, who was a few years older than our kids, pulled them all along in a row as I snapped a few pictures. They were having a ball!

I started to prepare supper, and opened up a bottle labelled "mixed." When preparing my food, whatever was left over I tossed into a couple of jars, so we were interested in how it turned out. It was really good. Keith lit a fire for the kids to toast marshmallows.

We were having fun and chatting the evening away when one of the kids shouted, "What's that over there?"

"That's a bear," Bruce said. "He must be attracted by the smells of food."

Sure enough, it was a black bear trying very hard to find a way to get across the river. Fortunately for us, the current was very strong on that side of the river. The bear didn't get into the water. We all ran to the water's edge to get a closer look as he meandered down river. It was so exciting for the children to see a real bear close up. Were they worried? I think not, but to be on the safe side it was a wonderful opportunity for Keith to give the boys a shooting lesson. "Just in case," he said.

Bruce, Dorcass, and their youngest son Danny took their boat and followed the bear along the river, but the sound of the engine frightened him into the woods. We had had an exciting evening: the kids swam until their skin wrinkled, and the bear across the river was an experience the children would not soon forget. Bruce and his family needed to be home before dark, so after scaring the bear back into the woods with his boat, they continued on down river and on home from there.

After breakfast the following morning we went for a boat ride, and then because it was such a gorgeous day we decided to go up river on our float boards. Keith and Mark and I used the double air mattress while the three bigger kids each used their own floaters. There was no current in this part of the river. After lunch we went right back swimming. It was over twenty-eight degrees Celsius and extremely hot with the burning hot sand reflecting the heat back unto us. I was grateful that we'd taught the kids to swim. They thoroughly enjoyed the swimming area we had prepared for them. The cool water of the river was very refreshing.

Later that evening I finally got everyone settled down. It had been an exciting day. With the company of family and a bear practically on our doorstep, it was no wonder the kids couldn't get to sleep. Who said camping is restful?

Bruce returned to our campsite the next afternoon for a visit with three other kids; his sons Larry and Danny and a friend whom I didn't know. They stayed until almost suppertime, then he went back to pick up his wife Dorcass. They returned with a fresh salmon. I stewed it for supper. It was delicious! Of course the kids went back swimming after supper. It was still very warm. Bruce decided to go fishing for pike, but he didn't catch anything, even though the day before, just at the water's edge, we could see huge pike cooling in the shade of an overhanging tree. We then lit a fire so all the kids could toast marshmallows. It was almost dark when they finally left. Now we had to get the kids settled down and prepared for bed. It sure was another fun day.

On July 19th we woke up to another beautiful day, sunny and warm. We went swimming before breakfast, then returned to prepared cold cereal, as it was too hot to light the stove. We then went for a boat ride up the river. We returned and cooked hot dogs for lunch. After lunch I was feeling sleepy so I went for a nap. Afterward, I had enough energy to clean out the tents. The kids went swimming and Keith played the guitar for a little while. I thought it was too chilly for the kids to stay too long in the water, so we took a walk around the island. After supper we toasted marshmallows again, and had a little sing-song. Finally, off to bed.

A few days later I said to Keith, "We'll have to go to Goose Bay today to shop for the weekend and run some errands."

"Alright. I'll need to pick up gas for the generator."

We piled into the boat and headed for civilization. We shopped and picked up some groceries and gas. By the time we returned to camp the temperature had warmed up with the afternoon sun. As usual the kids wanted to go swimming, but we wouldn't allow them because it was still too chilly. Keith had picked up his golf clubs and proceeded to make himself a three-fairway golf course, complete with numbered flags. One didn't have to worry about losing the golf balls in the river because there was lots of room. That's not to say we didn't lose a few, mind you. It was a wonderful way to get exercise. We all played a round of golf that evening.

The next day Mark found a large safety pin, so we decided to try to catch the pike that were always resting under the trees overhanging our swimming hole. We didn't have sufficient fishing equipment, but Keith put it all together so Mark could try his hand at fishing, more so in fun then actually fishing. The pike were so large that little Mark would have been pulled into the river had he snagged one.

Everyone went swimming after lunch. The water was warmer than the air. While we were swimming, we looked up and saw a boat approaching. It was Bill Carson and his son Dave, along with a couple of friends. We welcomed them and dug out a couple of cold beers from our stash deep in the ground and mixed us a couple of drinks. They were impressed with our refrigeration system. Mr. Carson was manager of the Hudson's Bay store in Happy Valley. His son Dave played in a local band. I played my accordion and Greg played his guitar. We had a sing-song with everyone joining in. Dave was really amazed with Gregory's talent for music.

"I would be surprised if Greg's not playing in a band by the time he's fourteen years old," Dave said.

Our guests stayed until dark. Dave stole a couple beers from us and left for Muskrat Falls for the night. He promised to return the beer the following day. We then got the kids settled for bed. The following morning, true to his word, Bill came back with a case of beer. We sat and chatted for a few minutes and he left. I gazed out over the river, paused for a moment, and took a deep breath of Labrador's clean, fresh air.

There was a boat coming to our island. We all ran down to see who it was and to greet them. It was Don Mitsuk, a local friend, with his girlfriend. We entertained them until late afternoon, including a feed of stew, which they enjoyed immensely. The kids went swimming again, then supper, then a walk around the island. After supper, we had a putting contest until dark. We ended our day tired, but content.

The following day it was warm enough even for me to go swimming. I was a little fussier about water temperatures than the children. I had a long swim and frolicked with the kids all morning. Early afternoon I lay in the tent and read for a while because I was exhausted from such an active day. I was in the middle of a story when I heard Keith hollering.

"What?" I hollered back.

"Nina is across the river yelling at us to pick her up."

I dropped everything! Nina had been one of my best friends for years, my swimming companion so to speak, and I was ecstatic she would want to visit for the evening. I ran to the water's edge and we waved at each other.

"Keith is coming for you," I yelled.

"I may not be able to get my engine started," he said.

I was anxious and worried for a few moments, but it did start, and Keith scooted across the river to pick up Nina and her two beautiful daughters, Kimberly and Michelle. I was so happy to see my friend. We raced along the beach while Keith went to fetch them. Our children were happy to have friends to play with. Nina brought a drink for us and we had a relaxing afternoon watching the kids play and race along the beach. Suddenly it got cloudy. In Labrador the weather can change extremely quickly and it started to rain. It poured from the heavens for a short while. The kids came running into our tent.

"Mommy, the rain is coming in our tent."

"Where from? The roof?"

"No, the window," Greg said.

Keith went to fix the problem and all was well again. Greg played his guitar and we all had a sing-song, which entertained us through the rainstorm, then they ran outside again while I made popcorn. They were happy. I wanted Nina to stay for supper; the girls wanted to stay the night and our kids wanted them to as well. Unfortunately, they had to go, but they promised they would return the following day. Keith was concerned about the engine starting, but it did and off they flew across the river, back to civilization.

Just as we were trying to get the kids to settle down for the night we heard a helicopter, and it sounded like it was coming really close, so we ran outside to investigate. It was so low we thought it was going to touch down on our beach. As we were running towards it waving our arms, it took off. We were puzzled as to why it came. There may have been a report of a family stranded on a beach in the middle of the river. However, when they saw a bunch of happy, smiling faces running towards them and waving, they probably decided that there was no one in distress here and took off before we could take any pictures.

On July 21st, I woke up to the delicious smell of bacon and eggs cooking. Greg and Darlene had made our breakfast. I was so proud of them. I had had a good night's sleep, so I decided to do the laundry by hand. It was no easy task, as I hadn't hand-washed anything for years. However, it was a good feeling to see it flapping in the wind on the clothesline Keith had put up for me. I then decided to clear out the main tent. I emptied everything out and turned the rug around. I'd laid it down to cover the sandy floor. I cleaned everything before putting it back inside. I had all my work done by early afternoon and was able to go lifeguard for the kids. They were never allowed to go swimming without one of us to watch them.

On July 23 we woke up early with the sun streaming in the tent windows. We were going to have a party for Darlene's birthday. It was also Michelle's birthday, and they planned to return for a birthday bash later on. The weather promised to be ideal. It remained sunny and warm with cotton-ball clouds floating throughout the beautiful Labrador sky. I cleaned out the tents while Keith watched the kids swimming. I decided to put some salt beef and spareribs on to boil for a few hours while it was still cool enough to cook. Then, while our guests were here we could enjoy their company instead of having to watch the pot. Early afternoon, I eagerly awaited our friends' shout from across the river. Sure enough, about two in the afternoon we heard them and Keith wasted no time pushing the boat into the river to fetch them. The children were so excited and kept jumping up and down and racing along the beach. Nina was bringing the birthday cake for both girls.

As Keith approached our beach with his precious cargo I was delighted to welcome them. I got us a drink from the in-ground refrigerator and took the kids to the roped-off swimming area. We swam and basked in the sun until four o'clock.

"I'm starved, Josie," Mike yelled.

"Me too," Keith piped up.

Darlene holding an umbrella during our camping trip to Willow Island on the Churchill River, 1973.

Nina and I went into the tent to peel vegetables, specifically carrots, turnips, potatoes, and cabbage, and placed them into the pot with the partially cooked ribs. It smelled so good! Now all we had to do was to wait for the veggies to cook. We told the kids to come out of the water and they grumbled at having to do so. I'm sure they would like to stay in the water around the clock, but we wanted to entertain our friends. As we sat around the tent, the kids had fun drawing on the beach and playing golf. Mike got too hot, so he took the scissors and cut off a good pair of jeans. Keith followed suit and cut off his good jeans, ruining them completely! How could he have made such a mess? We had a wonderful afternoon watching the kids frolic on the beach, wrestling and having fun. Keith and Mike played a round of golf. Nina and I were getting tipsy from the wine. As we prepared the table for supper, I was thinking how fortunate we were to have such wonderful friends and a phenomenal life. Supper was finally ready and it was delicious. We were just about to cut Darlene's and Michelle's birthday cake when Mark shouted, "Where's the boat?"

We all looked. Sure enough, the boat was missing from its usual spot on the beach. Looking further, we saw it was rapidly floating down river. This was serious, as it was our only way off the island. Keith wasted no time donning a life jacket and a float board. On that part of the river the current was very strong so he was quite nervous, and we were very anxious for him. He needed to get to it before it reached the deepest and strongest current. Once he finally reached it he jumped aboard, drove her back, and pulled her well up onto the beach. That was a close call!

"Can we have our cake now, Mommy?" Darlene asked.

"Oh yes, cake! We have to get the cake," I said, as much to myself as anybody else.

It had been a great day and now our friends were ready to go home. As we hugged and parted we were tired but happy. I wondered what tomorrow would bring.

The next morning was cloudy and damp. There was a low pressure coming in, which meant rain in the forecast, so we decided to pack up and return home. I took a while to repack everything and carry it to the boat. It reminded me of when my parents had to move twice a year from our summer home to our winter dwelling further in the bay. Now, as it was then, it was no easy task and it took a while to get everything to the beach. Everyone did their share of lugging and slugging supplies. There was no beer or soft drinks and very little food left. Even so, we still had to make two trips in the boat to get all our supplies across the river, then two trips in the car and finally back home.

I'll never forget that camping trip, with its sun-filled days of doing nothing but swimming, eating, and enjoying our family and friends. Watching the kids swim until their skin wrinkled, seeing them enjoy a round of golf with their father, and him teaching them how to fire a rifle when the black bear came across the river warmed my heart as never before. In just one week we experienced so many events! Keith's brother and family visiting, Mr. Carson dropping by for a visit, the helicopter investigating to see if we were all right was exciting. Then there was the girls' birthdays, it all added so much to one week of vacationing on the mighty Churchill River in Labrador. We'd been fortunate enough to enjoy excellent weather, the food that I had preserved in mason jars so I wouldn't have to cook each night was a hit, and it was very important to make sure the fly repellent was handy at all times.

I will see it in my mind's eye forever, the moon rising across the water, and the stars so brilliant they lit up the whole sky. And in the morning when the river was so still and so calm it reflected the river bank, the pointed spruce trees and clouds, like a giant mirror casting double beauty everywhere … we would have to do this again.

Later that summer, Keith and I took one more trip up the river in our little red-and-white-striped boat. We found a place where the river was calm enough to land the boat and we walked as close to the mighty Muskrat Falls as we dared. It was an amazing experience to see the power of this river as the water gushed over the falls.

"I'd hate to fall into that river," I said.

"Ya, you wouldn't last long in there."

I can't remember what happened to that little boat. As for the jet ski Keith built? We just left it on the island.

Chapter 32

Kool Kat Five

Dave Carson had been right about Greg having his own band by the time he was fourteen. Greg turned thirteen in July of 1974. He'd learned to play right away and in a few weeks was jamming with a couple of kids from the area. We were so impressed with his skill in music that his dad decided to have Gregory start up his own band. Greg selected John Greenleaves on guitar, and one adult, Gus, who had heard the kids play and wanted to join them. He was their first drummer. A short time later, a lovely young boy, Paul Patey, joined the group as drummer, and Gus stepped down. Daren English joined the group as another guitar player. He was the son of Joe English, who owned the most popular band in town. Gregory was the band leader. I was bandmaster and made sure they practised every day after school in our garage. They called themselves the Kool Kat Five. A few weeks later, three very talented girl singers, Brenda Blakeney, Donna Churchill, and Nathlyn Jones, joined the group. They added a formidable presence to the band. There were now seven of them. Eventually, they started getting bookings to play all over the community.

After the girls joined, we tagged on the Kool Kat Five plus Two, but the group decided that Kool Kat Five was sufficient, as they were already recognized by that name. They played a lot of Creedence Clearwater Revival, the Beatles, Neil Diamond, Meat Loaf and many top songs of the seventies. Greg would listen to the radio, and if he thought he could do a certain number, he would practise until he had it. It was such a joy to see them so wrapped up in their little band and enjoying the music. Children of all ages came from all over for a Saturday afternoon performance. The Kool Kat Five were to become a hot item on the Goose for several years. Gus Joshua, a talented local musician, said of Greg's talent: "Young Greg is more successful than he knows."

There was one event when Greg got to play with Joe English's band as a replacement for one of the players. He was only fourteen and rather nervous playing in an adult group. However, Joe must have had confidence that he could keep up. While on stage, Greg noticed that Joe's guitar was slightly out of tune. They were the most loved and respected musicians in Goose Bay. Gregory was not the type, nor was he in a position, to correct

Kool Kat Five, circa 1972–73. L-R: Donna Churchill, John Greenleaves, Nathlyn Jones, Paul Patey, Daren English, Brenda Blakeney, Gregory Penny.

the most popular band leader in town, therefore, he just kept on playing. One of Greg's group's most requested numbers was the hit "Wipe Out." Another popular number I enjoyed was "The Lion Sleeps Tonight." They played the latest seventies songs, both rock n roll and country, along with a few contemporary tunes as well.

Keith was still the sports representative for the Squirrel Club, therefore he was able to book the band there on Saturday afternoons. It didn't take long for word to spread, and pretty soon the club would be crowded with little kids wanting to hear them play. They also played at the sock hops, school dances, and the parish hall. But, the most memorable one for them was when they received a booking in the new high school in Natuashish, an Innu community on the opposite side of North West River. The girls went *crazy* for the boys in the band! They almost dragged our drummer Paul out of the car window. It was definitely a memory-making event. The kids said "it made us feel like *real* pop stars." They loved it!

They'd been playing hard for a couple of years and I thought they deserved some recognition for their talent. I phoned the Arts and Culture Centre in St. John's, Newfoundland. I told the gentleman how hard they'd worked and how popular they'd become. He was interested! We got the band a booking at the Arts and Culture Centre in March 1976. The group were ecstatic about their upcoming trip. They were going to the big city! We practised their repertoire every day and worked so very hard to get each number perfect. I had a local seamstress make costumes for them and we were all ready go.

On the day they were booked to fly out there was one of the biggest storms of the year. At Goose Bay Airport all flights were cancelled! I need not elaborate on the extent of their disappointment. Up to that point, the Kool Kat Five was one of the youngest musical groups ever to get a booking at the Arts and Culture Centre. However, after the initial disappointment they continued to perform. They looked pretty cool in their new on-stage costumes during local events. Moreover, many people were extremely impressed with their talent, and we were so very proud of our son.

Chapter 33

Living the Good Life

In 1975, Keith was still working for the Ministry of Transport as acting runway foreman and heavy equipment operator. It was a civil service job, which meant it was secure and stable. He was making good money. The problem was he never brought much of it home. He gambled it or drank it away. However, because I was working our children didn't want for anything.

I was making enough money with my two franchises, Dixie Lee Chicken and Elmer's Pizza, to afford us a good quality of life. I had staff working my pizza shop and chicken franchises. I also operated the kitchen and dining room at the Squirrel Club every Saturday night. On special occasions, we would have roast beef dinners or lobster dinners. I helped another friend to cater wedding receptions and banquets as well. My best friend, Emcee, came to help me cook and serve the customers. I also helped other friends with their catering events at the officers' club or sergeants' mess during military formals. There could be as many as eighteen pieces of dinnerware per setting!

Keith had been sports representative for the Squirrel Club for the past several years, which pleased him greatly because he could drink all the alcohol he wanted for free. It seemed he couldn't get enough. I prided myself in not being a nagging wife. I'd learned early on in our marriage not to do that. Many a black eye, busted lip, and broken furniture taught me to hold back and not upset him further.

I tried to keep the house and family together as best I could and struggled to keep four very active children on the right track. Gregory was getting good grades in school, Darlene was average, Cathy was doing excellent, and Mark, being dyslexic, struggled to keep up. Our sons were not interested in team sports, such as baseball and hockey. But in individual sports·such as swimming, golfing, skiing, they excelled and did exceptionally well.

Over the course of several years I'd hired different live-in housekeepers to take care of my home and family while I worked. On their days off and sometimes in the evenings we hired people. Therefore, I'd had some questionable babysitters on occasion. Not knowing it at the time, our daughters were molested by young male babysitters. I'd had no idea! Our daughters felt too ashamed and they didn't know how to tell me. They never told me until after we moved to Ontario. I wish I'd known it at the time that it happened. There would have been hell to pay! It broke my heart all over again.

Keith had always been a dreamer, an inventor, an artist, and occasionally came up with a new invention or new idea to make a lot of money. We bought a big boat and his intention was to gut it and rebuild it into a fancy cruiser. It never materialized. Then he bought a small runabout, and remodelled it in the basement of our house. We barely got it up through the stairway. We did enjoy it for one summer. He then built the jet ski I mentioned earlier, which I thought was pretty cool. However, getting it manufactured or to market was way beyond our financial capabilities. Every year there would be a new scheme of some kind.

Keith and I had become a part of the happy gang, the socialites and the party groupies of the seventies. We were at the club almost every Saturday night or we were at a house party of one of our friends. Emcee and Ray were our closest friends. Then there was George and Eleanor,

Dave and Marie, Ned and Theresa, plus several other friends from the motor pool. We were also friends with several of the pilots of Labrador Airways. Mike and Nina were close friends. Nina was my swimming friend. She was beautiful, tall and slim, unlike myself at barely five foot. Tom and Peggy Simms were friends. I once went on a flight with Tom as pilot; I was in the co-pilot seat. We gorged on a case of grapes in a box between us. Other pilot was Joe Gibbons, and his wife. There was also Ian Massie, son of the Mrs. Massie from Cartwright whose mom I'd worked for in Cartwright when I was eleven years old. I also had several swimming friends. When we were high on alcohol it became easy to forget the hardships of earlier times. It flowed freely during those good times. Keith was a prankster and we would hear wild stories of tricks he'd played on his co-workers. We laughed a lot and had a lot of fun. We were young and carefree.

I regularly played several rounds of golf during the short summers, and I played cards for a while during the wintertime. I visited with my friend Emcee when my busy schedule of work and other commitments would allow me the time. I felt the sting of rejection when my best friend had one of her girlfriends from her hometown in Nova Scotia living in Goose Bay. Her husband had been stationed on the Goose with the Canadian Forces for a year. I was glad when they left. We'd been close for many years and I missed her friendship terribly. But when we talked later, she told me she'd felt the same rejection when I started swimming with Nina.

All in all though, we'd moved into a comfortable lifestyle. A comfortable living and our children were settling in quite well and adjusting to the *Canadian* way of life, which was alien to the way I'd grown up on the Labrador Coast.

Chapter 34

Insanity

What drives people to do the things they do? I kept thinking that instinct played a very big part in how I lived my life, how I raised my children, and how I carried myself in public. Instinct is about not being able to think and just doing what needs to be done. Depersonalized people lose all trace of who they are, have no sense of self, feel unworthy, and are incapable of expressing their feelings. Many depersonalized people live their lives on instinct. I knew what needed to be done to raise my children to be responsible and caring adults. I wanted to do everything perfectly. I wanted to clean the house just so. There were programs on television that kept telling me what to do. Television shows, such as *Leave it to Beaver*, in a very subtle but effective way caused me to look at the way I was treating my children.

I could hear my mother's words ringing in my head:

"If you're going to do a job, do it right," she said. However, I found myself in a position where I felt I was doing it all wrong. Without realizing it, I was married to an insecure and disturbed man. I was very disturbed as well. I was the follower and this led to many problems. I was unable to say no, and being a people pleaser for most of my life was my undoing.

The old fashioned way of treating children was that they should be seen and not heard. However, it seemed no longer popular. I was unable to express my love for our children and was incapable of showing affection or how I truly felt. Through pure grit, determination, and common sense, I knew what to teach them in terms of manners, being polite, courteous, and kind. I knew instinctively what to do, but fell short on the affection required for their emotional well-being. I'd been trained from early childhood to work. Because I had to work in order to care for my children's physical needs, they suffered a price: I was seldom home.

Keith was not there for the children either. He was the youngest of a large family and was unfamiliar with babies and small children. He did the only thing he was familiar with, which was being indifferent and staying away. I knew he wanted to be a more involved father, but because of his drinking and his fear of rejection from them, he was at a loss as to do. I loved him regardless. I saw a side of him that was endearing and kind, soft hearted and sensitive, unlike the tough exterior he displayed when with his buddies. He was riddled with fear and it just didn't fit how he wanted the rest of the world to see him.

My life involved coming home after work, having dinner, entertaining the children when I had the time, making sure they did their homework, and then spending time alone after the children went to bed. When I returned home late at night, I enjoyed my aquariums; it soothed me and calmed me down.

Keith could go in an instant from a laughing, fun guy to sudden anger and madness. He was out of control. When angry, he would pick up whatever was close by and smash everything in sight. We had to go without clocks, radios, and lamps for periods of time because he would hurl them against the wall. If I was the offending party, it could easily be me who was thrown against the wall. How had I allowed the craziness and physical abuse to go on for so long? I'd come to realize I was trapped in a lifestyle in which I had no control, and no means of escape.

In reality, my life had become the opposite of what I'd hoped it would be. My ideal life, as I'd come to learn from the television shows I watched, was nonexistent. My efforts were in vain because of the drinking and the busy lifestyle we were living. I wasn't aware that I had developed a problem with alcohol. I did realize that when Keith took me out on a Saturday night I always passed out or blacked out. When I drank too much, I became a flirt with a know-it-all-attitude. It was not one of the most pleasing attributes one could acquire. It caused many arguments and chaos in our home.

Work was my saving grace. I was doing a good job, and receiving many compliments. The praise gave me a wonderful feeling of gratification. It kept me relatively sane. In the process of trying to impress my friends and "keeping up with the Joneses," so to speak, work and social life took precedence over my family. As long as we could pay the babysitter, we were out with our friends. I left my children with strangers way too often. I wanted to be the perfect wife and mother, and I wanted to be the perfect worker. However, I felt I was failing in the most important job of all — mothering our children.

Even though I made enough money to run the household and meet the daily needs of my family, we were always broke. I carried hundreds of dollars around in my pockets and purse. Yet, when it came to summer holidays, we couldn't afford to go anywhere. It was difficult to pay the bills each month. Where did the money go? The more I seemed to make, the faster it seemed to disappear. Through drinking, clubbing, gambling, and spending beyond our means, we'd become power-hungry, selfish, and irresponsible parents.

Was I insane? That's a very good question indeed. I will continue to do my best with whatever energy, knowledge, and sanity I have left.

Chapter 35

Labrador Coastal Service

In earlier times, while the rest of the world took trains, planes, and all manner of road, rail, and air travel for granted, Newfoundland and Labrador still relied heavily on the sea for transportation. There was much talk along the coast that the beloved *Kyle* might be retiring. Even though all Labradorians loved the old steamer, it was time for her to go. Newer and more efficient ships with high-powered engines would now replace her.

In 1975, CN Marine commissioned a ferry, the *M.V. William Carson*, for the North Sydney to Port aux Basques run. In 1976 she was assigned to the Newfoundland-Labrador run between Lewisporte, Newfoundland, and Goose Bay, Labrador. She was built at the Vickers shipyard in Montreal, and was the first ferry to enable vehicles to drive on and off through a side door. She was capable of carrying 500 passengers and 104 vehicles. The service was long overdue and much appreciated by weary passengers who were now able to drive their vehicles straight onto the ferry. The old way of hoisting vehicles up onto the deck and strapping them down had finally become obsolete. The *William Carson* was an excellent ship for her time: fast, roomy, and comfortable.

In the summer of 1976 I decided to take a trip home to Cartwright to visit my family, without the children. They were taken care of by Dotty, my live-in housekeeper. I trusted they were in good hands. A few weeks prior, I'd shipped a living-room suite home to my mother that we no longer needed because a house we'd recently moved into was fully furnished. About the same time the federal government had several houses built for certain people in Cartwright and other communities along the Labrador Coast who met specific criteria. Gratefully, my mother qualified. Therefore, a new house was constructed next door to the old one at the bottom of Cartwright harbour.

I hadn't seen my family in several years, and I felt drawn to them. It was a trip I would remember forever. My mother was very proud of her new home. It had two bedrooms, a living room-kitchen combination, and a three-piece bathroom complete with running water.

I offered to wash the dishes after supper one evening. The water had always been heated in a tank attached to the wood stove. As I flipped the lid to dip the water out, Mom looked at me kind of odd.

"Whass ya doin, maid?" she asked.

"I'm getting water to wash the dishes," I replied.

"Turn on the tap and you'll get all the water you wants," she grinned.

"Oh yah," I said. "I'm so happy for you, Mommy."

Mom took me out to the old house next door that Daddy had built in 1953. She'd been proud of it then. I marvelled at how a family of ten could fit into such a tiny space. There was no electricity back then, just oil lamps and one huge mantle lamp for the main room. I climbed the ladder and looked up onto the loft where my sisters and I had slept on the floor in what looked like bins. One-by-twelve inch pine boards were used to separate our spaces. Mom had stitched flour sacks together and filled them with feathers for mattresses to fit into each one. One tiny window in the peak of the house had been our only source of light.

In my parents' room above her bed *the* shelf was still in place. It was where Mommy kept her treasures. It was empty now; but I was always curious as to what was up there, but afraid to look. I will never know what had been kept there. The outside porch also had a loft where she hid food out of our reach. When Daddy got paid I knew there would be goodies tucked away in special hiding places. When we were little, whenever I got the chance, I would climb up to steal a few cookies or candies.

There were two porches. The inside porch served as a second kitchen and was also used for food storage. The huge nail was still in the wall beside the old comfort stove, where Mommy hung a whole bologna. I got in trouble many times for digging out a huge chunk to munch on.

I could visualize all of Daddy's gear hanging on huge nails in the wall of the outer porch. His dog harnesses, his bridle and traces, his guns and snowshoes — each had its own nail. I recalled the pile of unplucked birds hanging on those nails. After a successful hunting trip they would be piled onto the floor as well. In the dead of winter they remained solidly frozen with the feathers still on them.

As we continued through the house, my eyes filled with tears. Memories of the life we'd had here, some happy, some tragic, came flashing back. I was in awe as I gazed around the old shack: the pitiful shelves that held our dishes, the nail in the wall where Mom had hung her sewing needle cushion, the sturdy shelf that held up the radio and the six-volt battery that powered it. My sniffling continued as I looked up through the stovepipe hole into the loft. It was where I listened to our parents and their friends playing cards and laughing well into the night. Situated around the stovepipe, the lines once suspended from the ceiling to hang wet clothes on were gone. I could still see Daddy's sealskin mukluks hanging there. They would dry hard and stiff and Mom had to pull them back and forth on a stick shaped at the top end similar to an axe blade to soften them. As we entered the main room, there was the bench locker along one wall that held the wash basin on one end, and above the basin the cardboard Rinso box that held our combs but was no longer there. The rest of the bench was used for seating, with lots of nails in the wall above it for hanging coats and parkas on. The one window on that side of the house faced the harbour. The window on the opposite side faced the marsh, and beyond it the United States radar site on top of *Big Hill*. It was all so clear in my mind. Whatever the circumstances, we all grew up healthy and strong.

I had a long talk with my mother that day. I saw a side of her that I hadn't seen since we went to St. Anthony Hospital together when I was twelve. We'd flown in the Grenfell Mission plane to have my tonsils removed. She really was a gentle and caring person. As a selfish, spoiled child I couldn't see it. She'd never apologized for how she treated us as children and I never expected her to. Now that I was the mother of four, I understood, to some degree, why. Finally, I felt we had connected. I could see why so many people loved Aunt Flossie. It had been a meaningful and fulfilling trip.

As I was tearfully bidding my Mom and sibling farewell and telling them I would try to make it back real soon, the ship's horn made its first huge blast that vibrated throughout the community. The old *Kyle* had always given a warning blast to give passengers time to get out to her. I took it for granted there would be a second or third blast from the *William Carson*. I didn't know we had to board right away. I thought I had plenty of time to get up to the dock before she pulled out of port. Wrong! As I was saying my last goodbyes I looked out the window and the ship was turning around and heading out of the harbour. What do I do now? I was panicking because I knew I'd missed the boat — literally!

"I'll run you out to her," a friend of the family said.

"What will that do?" I screamed.

"I don't know, but tis worth a try," he replied.

I grabbed my things and we ran to the tiny speed boat pulled up in the cove. By this time, the ship was already turning around the point and picking up speed. She was headed straight out to sea. The little punt needed more speed if we were to catch her. Even at full throttle she would be hard to catch. I could see we were getting closer to her. She looked massive from our tiny boat as we sped along beside her.

No one had ever heard of a ship stopping for a small speed boat. Lots of little boats followed along beside them for short periods of time, either for sport or to bid a loved one goodbye. The *William Carson* was now full speed ahead. I was extremely distraught and started waving my arms and yelling at the top of my lungs. My neck was hurting from looking up at her and trying get the captain's attention. We were now just behind her and I kept yelling and waving my arms. Just as we were about to give up, the huge ship started to slow down! Was she really going to stop?

She was slowing down. Then I saw a gigantic hatch lifting up on the side of the ship. When she finally stopped, I couldn't believe what I was seeing. There was a huge hole in the side of her. It was about fifteen feet from where I stood in the tiny dinghy. How would I ever get up there? Along with my luggage, I was also clutching a loaf of fresh homemade bread Mom had given me as I was leaving.

Then I saw a rope ladder being lowered. I would have to climb up on that thing? I became more terrified as the ladder kept swinging and twisting its way down. But it seemed I would have no choice if I was to get home to my children. The ladder was dangling in front of me now and I had to climb onto it. I had no time to think, so I tossed my precious bread into the North Atlantic and grabbed my suitcase. With all the courage and brute strength I could muster, I grabbed the rope ladder and pulled myself onto it. My arms almost gave out as the ship swayed to and fro. I prayed I would reach the cargo hold. Exhausted, I fell onto the filthy floor and wept with relief. I could not believe what had just happened. I was then called to the captain's bridge and it was our friend Captain Kean. I was delighted to see him, and he was happy I'd gotten on board safely.

"I looked out the side door and recognized you," he said.

"Words will never explain how glad I am that you did," I replied.

"Not a lot of people get to stop a ship of this size for a single passenger," he reminded me.

"No, I guess not," I said, still shaking. I was speechless.

I got the strangest looks from other passengers as we sailed to Goose Bay and my family. I will be forever grateful to Captain Kean for stopping the ship and allowing me to get home to them.

My first introduction to Captain Jack Kean was when the *William Carson* was on her maiden voyage. Keith was working for Labrador Airways. They were sporting their new Labrador Airways crested jackets, and Jack thought Keith was one of the pilots. They struck up a conversation. Keith told him he was building a boat and needed a special kind of paint.

"I'll bring you back one on the next trip down," Jack told Keith.

As it turned out, Captain Jack Kean came to our house for dinner that night, and we got to know him quite well. The next morning Labrador

Airways took the captain and several local dignitaries on a short fishing trip into the Labrador interior. They flew in a Beaver, a bush-plane built by de Havilland.

On May 31, 1977, it was Captain Norman Hinks' turn to captain the *William Carson* as it left St. John's for Labrador. Though not the chief captain for this trip, Jack was on board as well. And he'd brought Keith's paint!

On June 2, 1977, on a calm summer morning, off the historical fishing port of Battle Harbour, the ship encountered a sharp iceberg a few feet below her waterline. Immediately the ship started to fill with water. Captain Hinks ordered a reduction in speed, but it was too late. A distress signal was picked up by the *Sir Humphrey Gilbert* in St John's. Lifeboats were lowered and filled quickly with distressed passengers. Our nephew Douglas Penny was on board when it sank. It was reported that the sound of the ice scraping the hull was deafening. Some of the lifeboats hadn't any motors on them, but the ones that did towed the terrified passengers out of danger, because the huge ship created suction as it went below the surface. This quick thinking prevented a bigger disaster. There were a couple of helicopters also on scene to airlift survivors to safety. All the passengers and crew survived. The generators were still running as she sank below the surface. A month later the *M.V. William Carson* was located in 504 feet of water.

The Labrador Coastal Service is still running today, even though the Trans-Labrador Highway is finally through from coast to coast. The *Sir Robert Bond* in the current ship servicing the Labrador coast.

Chapter 36

The American Side

In 1975, Keith was working as a parts manager for Labrador Airways. I was very angry at him for quitting a civil service job where there was security and stability for our growing family. Then he informed me we would have to move from our comfortable military housing.

"Now where do we go?" I shouted.

"I'll find us a place on the American side."

"American side?"

My mind was racing. I was thinking there was no way that could ever happen. Even though I knew the American military had been moving out in droves of late, I couldn't comprehend it. I had developed a mindset and was conditioned to think that the Americans were much too superior to allow civilians to live anywhere near where they lived, and that all civilians were much too inferior to live in their midst. Furthermore, even if we did get to move over there, wouldn't our children be bullied? I had always been conscious of that. However, I kept hearing that civilians were moving to the American base, but never thought it could ever happen to us. Was I the only one feeling that way?

Keith went ahead and applied for a house in the 1100 area of the American base. The housing complex was built for families with children. It had semi-detached housing and row housing. We ended up with a duplex. When I walked in, I was amazed at the space. There were five bedrooms: one for each of our children and a huge master bedroom for us. However, we gave the girls the master bedroom, and they were delighted. I went about unpacking — again! The house came already furnished, so there wasn't much to do. I was pleased that I only had to buy groceries. The children each unpacked their belongings, and I noticed they had very little to unpack. Maybe they did have enough, but they just had more space to put it in. I couldn't help but think of the winter we'd been forced to move into the basement of the new house Keith had started building. There'd been eight of us, including my sister Sal and her son Steven, crammed into an environment not fit for human beings. Now here we were. Was this real? Could we actually live here? I was in awe; not only was this a great space for our growing family, but I had my sister Sal and her family across the street. The property backed onto a field and forest where the children had plenty of room to play.

I still was not content. Something deep down was troubling me. Suddenly, it became crystal clear. We had to sell our business! I finally accepted the fact that the American military would be moving out. The process was already happening all around us. I felt our business would not survive without the American military to support us. They loved their pizza.

One night after a long talk about what to do, Keith and I made the gut-wrenching decision to sell the pizza shop and the chicken franchise. But, who would want to buy during such uncertain times? I had two Volkswagens, plus I'd recently bought myself a 1970 Chevy Impala from an American for one hundred dollars. I was too wrapped up in my struggle with the business to pay much attention to the gossip of the base closure. But it would not go away, and we were terrified for our family. After all, we had four growing children! With much trepidation and fear, we finally decided to put an ad in the local paper to sell both franchises.

Memories kept rushing back as to how we got started, of all the hard work of keeping them running and I wondered if any of it had been worth it. What had we gained? I was riddled with fear at the prospect of having to sell. After just a few weeks, both franchises sold. We were ecstatic, but what would I do now? It took several weeks to get the business affairs settled and I was free to do whatever I wanted. It felt strange not to have to go to work. I decided to enjoy the summer and took the children swimming, golfing, and picnicking.

After getting settled, I went about trying to find a job for the winter. Rumours were flying around that the officers' mess was cutting down on civilian staff and laying off people who had worked there for years. Something big was in the works, but nobody was saying anything.

Living in a small town one can appreciate the lifestyle, but also once a reputation has been established, either good or not so good, it can stick around for many years. I don't even care to think what mine might have been. I know that where my work was concerned my reputation was good. My mother taught me good work ethics. What I'd learned then, stayed with me throughout my life. I'd been a business owner for the past seven years. I'd worked hard and maintained those qualities throughout. Therefore, when the U.S. military was looking for someone to fill a special position, my name must have come up. I was called in to the officers' mess for an interview.

"Mrs. Penny, we have a delicate situation here, and we realize this won't be a comfortable position to put you in, but this job calls for a competent person to fill a somewhat awkward position."

"Pardon, sir?"

"We would like to hire you as cook for the officers' mess. You will be in complete charge of everything that happens ... after we have let all our other civilian employees go."

"Pardon, sir? What do you mean?" I mumbled.

Suddenly fear shot through me. What was he talking about, letting everybody else go? I certainly didn't like what I was hearing. I knew most of these people. I would be despised and hated for this.

"This is what's happening," the sergeant tried to explain. I was all ears and my heart was about to jump out of my chest. "The base is closing down. We have to lay off all of our civilian employees. Therefore we need someone impartial, who has not worked here before, to see it through until closing."

"When will that be?" I asked.

"Within the next year."

I was speechless. This sounded like an important job, but risky as well. I was flabbergasted! They wanted *me*? My mind was racing. Even though I knew it would be difficult, I could not miss this opportunity.

"Yes, sir. I will do my best to do a good job for you. But why me?"

"During our search for the right person, your name kept coming up. Therefore we would like you to fill this position. We'll give you a few days to think it over."

"No, sir. I don't need a couple of days. I'll take it."

"Marvelous. I know you will do a good job for us."

"Yes, sir. I certainly will try, sir," I managed to say, as they shook my hand.

"You will work with the existing staff until you are trained, then we will start letting them go one by one."

I walked out of the office, still wondering what had just happened. I felt honoured, yet targeted and judged. It sounded like a fearsome responsibility. Could I do this?

I went home to my family and told Keith.

"Well they must believe you can do it. What will you have to do?"

"I was informed that the civilians will be let go one at a time until there is only me left."

"Then what?" he asked.

"They will keep several of the airmen as helpers. As the military personnel leave the base, there will be fewer people to cook for and fewer staff needed to feed them," I explained.

Of course, I was only speculating. I didn't know any more than anyone else what was really happening, or about to happen.

As I thought about the situation, I tried to convince myself that even though it would be uncomfortable, I would just forge ahead and do my job to the best of my ability. I started work shortly thereafter, and was issued my whites and introduced to all the staff. They hadn't been informed of what was happening, so they were full of questions, and I didn't have the answers for them. I had never felt so guilty in my life, even though it really had nothing to do with me. Some of the staff assumed what was happening, while others had question and fear in their eyes. After all, they'd been working there for many, many years. The rumours that had been floating around Goose Bay for the last couple of years came to light in cinemascope. The Americans were really going to move out, going to leave for good, going to abandon us! What would happen to all the people who'd built their lives here? Who'd moved here as young people and knew no other way?

However, once I got the job, reality began to sink in. Something big was about to happen in Goose Bay. By this time it was becoming evident that the rumours of the military leaving Goose Bay were true. I couldn't believe it, because the military *was* Goose Bay. If they moved out, what would be left? Would all of the Canadian troops be gone? Could all the United States troops be moving out? And would the British move out as well? The Royal Air Force had held a small contingency of troops on the base since 1942. Their lives were very restricted as to what they could do: no fraternization, they were not allowed to leave the base, they had to buy their alcohol from the PX, which they found rather boring, and no entertainment. Eventually, they got their own club on the Canadian side called the Bulldog Club and were able to drink their own liquor. I remember them being fiercely competitive during carnival time, but other than that, I never saw them. The only time we would miss them would be during the Winter Carnival. The thought of the base closing was hard to contemplate. Would there be no more super jets lined up along the airdrome? And what about the Canadian Armed Forces? Would they be moving out as well? Questions kept flying around town. There were too many questions without answers.

I started work at the officers' mess in the fall of 1975. The cooks took me into the huge walk-in freezers. My boss informed me that all the food currently in stock had to be cooked and served within a certain period of time or it would be thrown out.

"What? Thrown out?" I was shocked.

"Yes. Thrown out," he repeated.

"Why not give it to the locals?"

"No, it can't be given to the locals, or handed over to the needy or the Salvation Army, or any other organization that might be able to use it."

"Why?"

"It *has* to be thrown out! That's all I can tell you," he said.

He sounded as angry as I felt. There were so many people who could use this food! I was speechless. There were cases and cases of roast beef, ribs, sides of pork, steaks, and all manner of seafood: shrimp, scallops, salmon, and cod. I focused on keeping my mouth shut. I could be very brash or downright nasty if I saw something happening that ran against my principles. This was unbelievable! There weren't even enough personnel left on base, or even in Goose Bay, to eat all this food.

Putting all of that aside, I began training. I had never been in such an awkward position before. The civilians taught me how to use the oversized cooking pots, huge steamer vats, and ovens. I caught on quickly and soon I was able to operate the kitchen with confidence. It's strange to think back on how this actually happened. The staff was let go one at a time, as I'd been informed they would. Each week when I went in to work, somebody else would be missing. I felt terrible about this, but continued on with my work. What else could I do?

As the military personnel left the Goose, so did the staff from the officers' mess. Over the course of a few months, I was the only civilian left in the kitchen. It was then that the huge parties began. Every night for dinner we cooked elaborate dinners of prime rib roasts, porterhouse steaks, and filet mignon. The best of everything was served to the Canadian and American officers, along with prominent civilian residents and business men of Happy Valley–Goose Bay. I couldn't help but think of the hungry days I'd had growing up on the coast of Labrador. There had been many times when our people almost starved to death, and I'd heard stories of people who actually did. I was very conscious of keeping myself in check. I tried to be impartial and not judge anybody. However, when I saw the amount of waste at the end of this period, I became very frustrated and heartsick.

I was not sorry when the powers-that-be let me go. There were several large cases of food still in the freezers when I left. I knew I'd just finished a big job and I was satisfied that I had done a good job for them.

I was given an excellent reference. As a matter of fact, it was that reference from the Americans that prompted the Canadians to hire me. They wanted me to go back to work in the Canadian Forces' mess hall. I was ecstatic, because with working for the Canadian military I would get full benefits once again. Also, Sal and Rhoda had been working there for several years. I was so happy to be with them.

I signed on and was reminded that I could shop in their stores and was permitted to use all the sporting facilities on base once again. I'd been teaching swimming throughout this time, and never relinquished my instructor's certificate. Also, I still was able to work in the Squirrel Club kitchen/dining room on Saturday nights.

Times were definitely changing, and Goose Bay would never again be the same. What would happen to the civilian population? Where would they go? The base was slowly but surely shutting down. The plans were in place. The strict rules that regulated this all-important base were slacking off. Reality was setting in. Hundreds of civilians had homes back in Newfoundland and had plans to return. But what about the Labradorians who'd built their lives around the base? Would they return to the semi-nomadic lifestyle of bygone years? It appeared, in some cases, there was no other choice.

Chapter 37

New Ventures

In the summer of 1976, I had finished working in the American officers' mess and hadn't yet got a job with the Canadian military. In the meantime, I was offered an interesting position. An acquaintance of ours, Bill Cosh, owned and operated a fish camp at Park Lake in Labrador's interior. He'd asked me if I would go as a cook and camp manager. I'd never heard of Park Lake before or even a fish camp, and the idea sounded intriguing.

"Where is it?" I asked.

"It's a long ways inland and we have to fly in." *Fly in?* That piqued my interest.

"I'll give it a try," I said.

I hadn't any plans for the summer anyway, and the money was good. At that time the children were fifteen, fourteen, twelve, and ten years of age; old enough to fend for themselves for a short while, plus their father would be home after work.

"How long will I have to stay?" I asked.

"Each trip lasts from three to five days. Very few parties last a week or longer."

"A few days? Yes I'll go."

Bill went on to explain what my job entailed, and what I needed to bring with me. Once the plane dropped me and the guides off, we would be totally alone. I was looking forward to this new adventure. I wanted to take Pollution with me. He would protect me from all danger.

A few days later, on a beautiful sunny morning, I drove to Otter Creek along with my dog, three guides, and lots of food and supplies. The eight guests would arrive later in the evening. After loading the plane with all the gear, I climbed into the Beaver aircraft and squeezed into my seat with Pollution on my lap. *Why so much?* I thought. We flew over Labrador's beautiful but rugged terrain for forty-five minutes, and there was not a road in sight. *Where the heck is this place?* I thought. Eventually we came upon a huge lake.

"How big is this lake?" I asked Mark Blake, the guide sitting beside me in the plane.

"Ten miles long. I used to trap in here in the thirties," he replied.

"Really? My dad was also a trapper in the 1940s in Roaches Brook," I told him.

"This is a great place for people who like to fish," Mark said.

He told me that Park Lake had always been known for its huge lake trout and pike. Guests flew in from all across Canada and the United States to fish here. I will always remember the beauty that unfolded in front of me as the plane circled and prepared to land. This was a fisherman's paradise. Nestled on the edge of this ten-mile lake, surrounded by tall spruce, juniper, and fir trees, were five buildings. A large cabin for the guests, two smaller cabins, one for the cook, and one for the guides, a small shack to store fishing gear, and a tiny hut for cleaning fish. Several small boats were pulled up onto shore. Tethered to the dock in the lake was a huge steel cage for holding live trout. They were kept until the end of the pre-arranged trip when "the keepers" would be cleaned by the guides and packed for the fishermen to take back with them.

Everybody helped to unload the gear and tote it into the cabins. Pollution ran about sniffing everything. He was a very happy dog. Then

I realized why he was so happy. He was vigorously rolling on the ground and having a grand old time. However, upon closer inspection, I could see he was rolling in a rotten fish full of maggots! I'd always hated maggots, and I'd had more than one bad experience with them in my day. The maggots were all over Pollution, and the smell was nauseating. I was beside myself. This was not a good start to my new job. I threw Pollution into the lake and shampooed him. Then I had to almost drag him to my cabin, which was the farthest distance from the main cabins.

As I toted my things along a narrow pathway of moss and sticks, I was feeling a little nervous about being so isolated. I'd been informed earlier that black bears sometimes swam across from a nearby island. Maybe I had reason to be scared.

The tiny cabin contained a set of bunk beds, a small dresser, and a tiny window facing the encampment. The guests' cabin accommodated eight. There was a huge dining table that seated eight to twelve people. A wood stove graced the opposite wall, around which large lounging chairs welcomed the travel-weary guests. There was also a generator for electricity. The kitchen was well equipped and the bedrooms looked comfortable.

It was my job to make the fishermen feel welcome. After taking a few minutes to settle myself, I went to the main cabin and started putting food away and prepared the bar for our guests. When that was completed and they all had their cocktails, I then started preparing hors d'oeuvres. Once that was done, I had to start preparing dinner. One thing was for sure, the guests of this fishing expedition would *not* go hungry.

The meals consisted of prime rib, the very best steaks, pork chops, and, of course, freshly caught Labrador lake trout. The routine was to start with a full breakfast: fresh-brewed coffee, eggs, bacon, sausage, ham, pancakes, and always freshly caught pan-fried trout. Toasted homemade bread smothered with local redberry and blueberry jams finished the breakfast meal, and shortly thereafter it was time to prepare the fishermen, boats, and gear for a day on the water.

Out came the fanciest fishing gear I'd ever seen. It was unlike the oils skins and sou'westers of the coastal fishermen like my dad, who'd risked their lives to eke a living from the cod fishery. I couldn't help but compare it to my son's fishing pole with a safety pin as a hook that we'd used while camping one summer.

After I cleaned up from breakfast and made the guests' beds, I returned to my cabin to make mine. The screen had been torn off my window. I ran immediately to Bill. I suspected it had been a black bear and I was right.

"Don't leave any food lying around in your cabin," he said.

"But I'm scared to go back myself; it's a long way in the woods."

"They won't hurt ya, Josie."

"Then why did they rip the screen off the window? They must have been trying to get in!" I shouted.

"Ok then, you can stay in my room and I'll move to one of the guest rooms."

I was satisfied with that arrangement, therefore able to carry on with my work, always mindful of the presence of bears.

The fishermen didn't come back for lunch, which I was grateful for. It gave me a chance to make the beds, clean the cabins, and take stock of what to cook for dinner that night. I was free for an hour in the afternoon to do whatever I wanted. I took my dog for a swim, careful not to allow him to stray and dive into a maggoty fish. He soon swished out a couple of muskrats to chase, which made him happy. The fishermen returned at four with very little to show for their efforts. The catch and release rule was in effect, which meant the guests were permitted to bring back enough only for their daily consumption. The fish were placed in the cage until it was time to clean them. There were several beautiful trout swimming around in the holding cage. The guides cleaned them just before I cooked them for breakfast each morning.

I set up the wet bar in the main room, and then prepared a huge tray of hors d'oeuvres. Using a glass tumbler, I had cut round pieces of fresh homemade bread I'd made that morning, and dressed them with a little salad dressing, a slice of tomato, cheese, cucumber, and cold cuts. Very simple. But our guests, who probably hadn't had homemade bread, thoroughly enjoyed them. Then I proceeded to cook dinner.

Our guests were excited about their day and raved about the place: the weather, the number of hits on line, the experienced guides, and the beautiful surroundings. There were a few complaints about black flies and mosquitoes. They were reminded to always use their insect repellents, mesh hoods, or whatever they brought with them for protection. On their last day of fishing they were allowed to keep enough trout to fill their quota. The guides knew just where to take the eager fishermen each day, to entice their appetites for more fishing. More importantly, the experienced guides knew exactly where to take them for their last day of fishing on this trout-infested lake to make sure they got their quota.

All too soon, we were packing the small bush plane for the return trip to Goose Bay. Bill told me that I did an excellent job and asked if I could return the following week. This time I would be in charge of the whole place and not just the cooking.

I spent the weekend preparing my house and the children for my absence, and before I knew it, I was on my way back to Park Lake. I had decided to take my daughters with me this time, as I was nervous about being alone in my cabin. Also, it would give me an opportunity to teach them about the things in life that we didn't normally do at home: how to make a bed properly, how to prepare appetizers, how to set a correct dining room table, and how to serve our guests. I had learned those things while in Girl Guides in Cartwright and while working for the officers' mess in Goose Bay. Besides, I knew they would enjoy the surroundings.

As we flew across the country, it gave my girls a sense of space. They realized the vast size of Labrador. The rugged mountains brought them in awe of their homeland. As we touched down on Park Lake, I was careful to keep an eye on Pollution. I did not want him rolling in maggots again. I asked the girls to watch him while I was busy. They were a great help. Because this was only a four-day trip, I needed to teach them quickly all I knew in terms of hosting a group of millionaires and how to be a good hostess. These were valuable lessons at the time. Darlene was fourteen and Cathy was twelve. Although they were still quite young, they were old enough to understand what I was trying to achieve. It was also a way of keeping them out of trouble. Having the girls with me made it seem more like a holiday than work. I enjoyed teaching them and they were willing students. Pollution was such a joy as well.

I did my usual daily chores of providing my guests with the best possible meals and service. The routine was much the same for each group, so it became easier each trip and I felt more confident than the first time. The girls were instructed to stay away from the guests, not to bother them at any time. After all, they didn't come from thousands of miles away to be pestered by a couple of little girls.

The week went by quickly and we were soon packing the plane with the usual gear, plus the fishermen's quotas of fresh trout. It was a given, and a guarantee, that every fisherman would go home with his quota. I was pleased with the results of this trip. I met interesting people from a different class of individuals. I was not familiar with rich people, but when I had a few glasses of wine in the evening, at their request, of course, I felt I could talk to them like anyone else. They were interested in where and how I grew up. And they expressed how much they enjoyed my cooking.

My third trip into Park Lake that summer was different. Keith decided to come along as a guide. Mind you, he'd never been a guide before, he'd never been to Park Lake before, and he didn't like fishing! It wasn't that he didn't know how to use a rod and reel or to fly-fish, he just didn't care for the sport. He did know how to handle small boats well, and he was a good all-around guy it terms of the outdoors. He grew up in Newfoundland and Labrador after all, and had been around boats all his life. Therefore, the head guide, Mark, thought Keith would be an asset to the group. We decided to leave the children in care of a babysitter and headed for Otter Creek. Again, I was amazed at the volume of supplies. The little plane was packed to capacity as we wiggled our bodies into our seats and strapped ourselves in. I was happy to have my husband beside me. We could treat this like a vacation of sorts. We'd been married sixteen years up to that point and had little opportunity to go anywhere together, especially on vacation away from the children. Maybe I would see another side of him.

Bill had decided to leave me in charge of his camp for this trip, as he was unable to come along. Maybe that's why Keith decided to join us. As the tiny plane touched down on this trout-filled lake, I felt more confident about what I was here to do. The routine was generally the same in terms of preparing the site for the guests. We would have eight people arriving in the morning, a full house, and there was lots to do: make the beds with clean linen, prepare the rooms, start the generator, make lots of ice for drinks, cut firewood to feed the huge wood stove, put the food away, prepare the kitchen, clean and dust everything in the main cabin, and prepare the fishing gear, boats, and canoes. We were tired and retired early to our cabin. I was able to use it now and not be as fearful of the bears.

The following morning, the guests arrived on schedule. It was clear from the beginning that this would be a different party. I was concerned by the amount of alcohol our guests had brought with them. I was convinced that there were several gentlemen who were here to have a good time rather than to fish. It was mid-morning when they got themselves straightened away, therefore they decided to go fishing in the afternoon. I made a pot of soup for lunch, cleaned, and prepared the kitchen for the busy week ahead. Then I relaxed for an hour in the afternoon. Around four o'clock I did my usual routine of preparing the bar with ice and lots of different kinds of alcohol. There were unusual shapes and sizes of bottles I'd never seen before. I had a huge number of steaks and potatoes to roast for dinner. The guides were busy cleaning the trout for breakfast the following morning. Keith had a good afternoon with the guests and made friends with one of the men. The following morning, after a huge breakfast, this trip took a different swing. The gentleman named John, who Keith had guided the previous afternoon, had made a decision.

"We are *all* going fishing today!" he shouted, grasping his open shirt and sticking out his chest.

"Oh no, I can't go. It's against company policy," I replied. "I have too much to do."

"No, you don't have too much to do, because we are going to help you with your work. Then we are going fishing … you included," he insisted. "We're not moving until all of us are ready to go!"

I was flabbergasted. I didn't know what to say or do. I felt very uncomfortable for several reasons. I didn't want them in my kitchen. I felt it wasn't right to have our guests washing dishes, making beds, and cleaning out the cabins. However, there they were, doing just that. Afterward, when all the work was finished, I needed to be outfitted with a life jacket, fishing pole, and all that goes with it. Finally, all of our guests, five guides, and I, were set to go.

Each boat carried two fishermen and one guide. Keith, myself, and our feisty guest John were in one boat. He seemed to be in charge of this whole party. Keith took us out into the heavy current, and nestled the boat against a huge rock. One of the men accidently dropped his line into the water and immediately there was a trout on it.

"Boy oh boy, this is going to be a great day!" one of the men shouted over the rush of the water. As we were casting our lines into the river, John pulled a bottle of whisky from his sack.

"Every time we catch a fish, we'll have a drink," he said.

"That sounds good to me," Keith agreed. He'd never turn down that opportunity.

They were getting quite inebriated quickly, and it seemed the trout were biting as never before. Keith caught a trout. Instead of reeling it in, he decided to walk it to shore! With his hip waders filled to the brim, fishing rod over his shoulder, the line and trout in tow, he stumbled his way to shore, falling into the water several times. We were in stitches laughing. Then, John and Keith did the same thing with the next few fish. There was no thought of safety. The alcohol had taken over all reason. Mark the head guide was on shore yelling for us to get out of there, but they paid no attention. Thankfully, Bill wasn't on this trip, therefore the guys were free to break any rules they wanted. I had lost complete control.

Shortly afterward I hooked my line on the bottom, and not wanting to let the party know, I almost cut my fingers off trying to hold on to it. Finally, I had to let the line go. It flew into the river so fast it made a pinging sound. I felt terrible losing the man's expensive rod and reel. After an hour or so, the men concluded that they were dangerously drunk and that maybe they should get to shore. On the way back they decided to troll for the lost fishing line, and wouldn't you know, they hooked it and retrieved the rod and reel. I was so happy. Once on shore, all the other guests were thankful we were still alive. There was much talk and laughter of the day's adventures. It was understood by everyone that we'd put ourselves in grave danger. We got a tongue lashing from Mark, rumblings from the rest of the crew, and mixed responses from the guests. But all was well in the end. It was an experience all of us would remember for many years to come.

The following morning, right on schedule when the float plane circled and touched down on that pristine lake, I was, once again, in awe of the beauty all around me. I remembered my mother once saying when we'd moved from a tiny village of two families, into Cartwright: "Just put me back in the bush, I'll be happy there." Now I totally understood.

Chapter 38

A New Life

In the spring of 1977 the future for my family was uncertain. The base was closing, and even though we didn't work for the military, it would inevitably affect us. Keith was working for Labrador Airways. I had recently started a job back on the Canadian side. During my interview I was told that the Americans were impressed with my work. We were still living on the base in the 1100 area on the American side. Our children were now teenagers, except Mark, who was only ten.

Gregory was a whiz in school. He got excellent grades and was developing into a fine young man. He wasn't giving us any trouble in terms of rebellion or any other typical teenage issues. We were very proud of him. Darlene, though not as book smart as her big brother, was a good student. She was a rocker and when she was little she would rock and bounce her body off the back of the couch quite vigorously. I was concerned that she might have suffered some mild brain damage from the car accident. Could it be possible this was causing this odd behaviour? However, she was responsible, and she felt the need to keep her siblings in line. At times she would get very frustrated with them because they were sloppy and didn't pick up after themselves. Cathy was very smart as well. She didn't have to work at getting excellent marks on her report card. I sensed that she felt rejected due to the extra attention Darlene received from the car accident. Even though Cathy did not display rebellion at home, she just chose not to be there. She spent as little time at home as possible, and thought nothing of leaving for hours at a time. Mark's grades were a bit lower, and unfortunately we didn't know at the time that he might be dyslexic. I once saw a television show on the condition because I knew Keith was dyslexic, and I was curious as to whether Mark might be suffering from the same thing. When he first wrote his name backwards, my suspicions were confirmed; although, he was never officially diagnosed. He struggled with reading, but put anything mechanical in front of him and he was a whiz. He was a climber as well and liked to get to the next highest level, whether it was a tree, a fence, or a swing.

When we were certain the Americans were moving out, Keith and I had a long talk. What would we do? We figured the local economy would go to hell. We had already sold our businesses and were grateful for that, but what of the future? We had four growing children to get through school, college, and university, or at least to find sustainable work. Where would they work if we stayed here? There were very few jobs for civilians, all the jobs that had been held by the military bases could now be transferred wherever there was a slot available. There didn't seem to be anything coming up in terms of new companies coming in. Labrador Linerboard, which held so much promise when they first arrived, had already moved out. Therefore it seemed like a bleak future ahead for the whole region.

Shortly after our conversation, the Canadian Broadcasting Corporation phoned me.

"Is this Josie Penny?"

"Pardon me?" I asked. After seventeen years of living with mainlanders I'd learned etiquette.

"Ryan's Fancy is coming to Goose Bay to do a show, and we're looking for the best dancer to fill a slot."

"Me? You want me to dance for a CBC television show?" I stammered.

"Yes. We heard you were a good stepper, and because the current champion is pregnant and can't do it, you were our next choice."

I was dumbfounded and couldn't believe what I was hearing. The Ryan's Fancy band was made up of three Irishmen: Dermot O'Reilly, Denis Ryan, and Fergus O'Byrne. They immigrated to Toronto from Ireland in 1967 and started an Irish band similar to the well-known Irish Rovers. After relocating to St. John's they played together using a couple of different names before settling on Ryan's Fancy. They soon become very popular throughout North America after a regular gig at the Strand Lounge in St. John's. The Newfoundlanders fell in love with the band as well. So much so that CBC and Ryan's Fancy started the first prime-time television series out of St. John's. The trio travelled throughout the Atlantic Provinces including Labrador to entertain the hundreds of music-hungry locals. I made sure to tune in every week to catch their show.

"Okay then, I'll do my best," I stammered, not knowing what else to say.

"Alright then, you are booked. The organizers will contact you when they are ready."

I stood frozen in the middle of the floor, and then it hit me as to what they actually wanted me to do! I started to shake, laugh, and cry all at the same time. Little *me* was going to be on a television show! This was a big deal. Over the next few weeks I thought it a good idea to practise up. So, I put a cassette in and "stepped 'er down" right there in my own kitchen. If nothing else, I could tone up the old muscles a bit. I went to the Bay and bought myself new shoes. They needed to be the right ones. Two-inch heels with slip proof taps would suffice. I wondered where they would film the show, whether I would get to practise, and how much they would pay me. I thought at times I'd dreamt the whole thing. I'd been a dancer all my life. Not in the professional sense, I might add, but every time I was at the club and the right tune was played, I'd get "itchy feet," so to speak, and just have to get out there and dance. When we were attending house parties, our friends would ask me to dance for them. They enjoyed my dancing, and I loved the attention.

On March 10, 1977, I got another phone call. It was a representative from the show asking if I could be at Pardy's Store for the following day.

Pardy's Store was located on the corner from where we had lived on Grand Street. It was not what I'd envisioned as a place to perform my dancing debut. However, I was in no position to argue.

"Yes, I'll be there," I said, already shaking from fear. What had I gotten myself into? I wanted to know if it was a local show or whether it would go all across the country. I was reassured it was just a local show. For whatever reason, that made me feel better.

When Keith and I arrived at the store the following day, Ryan's Fancy and the CBC crew were there and there was a piece of plywood on the floor. Couldn't they have found a more appropriate place to air their show? Even though I was curious, I dared not ask. Keith was with me and took a seat on the back wall with his beer. There were several drinkers around the room. They were instructed to hide the beer bottles from the cameras once the filming started. After introductions all around, I was asked a few simple questions. How long had I been dancing? Where did I train? Had I ever danced for any other company or group before? The CBC had its equipment all set up and the lights were blinding. I tried to stay focused on what I was there for. The tiny room was packed with wires, lights, and musical instruments: a banjo, a guitar, a mandolin, a fiddle, and an accordion. There was also a flute and Fergie was excellent on the hand drum. He asked me if there was a particular tune I'd like.

"'Turkey in the Straw' or 'St. Anne's Reel,'" I replied. "They have the best rhythm for my type of dance."

"All right then, we can do those," he said in his strong Irish accent. "We'll play a few practise tunes and see if you like them."

"Okay then," I replied, shaking in my new high-heel shoes.

Then the music started playing. I was so thrilled because Ryan's Fancy played the old traditional tunes. They were the same tunes that my dad played on his accordion when I was little. It captured my heart, lifted my spirits, and heightened my energy. I would have danced on that plywood with or without cameras. Also on the show were Sam and Bertha from Nain singing an Inuit Lament in their native language and Mrs. Goudie with a talk of how she'd lived in earlier times. Then it was my turn. As the music started, I was signalled to the centre of the plywood. They started playing "St. Anne's Reel" as I stepped onto that plywood. I danced until my feet started to tire, then Fergie put down his drum and grabbed me for a short swing. I loved to swing with people who knew how to swing well. I was so happy and grateful I hadn't tripped over my own feet. I did it! Everyone cheered and it was over.

The next day Keith's brother George phoned us from Burlington, Ontario.

"We saw you dancing on the Ryan's Fancy show. You did good," George said.

"Thank you," I replied.

"Why don't you come out for a holiday in the summer?" his wife Jessie asked.

"That sounds wonderful. We'll try to make it out for a visit," I replied.

They'd seen the show on television! I understood it was only to be a local show. Suddenly I was finding out it had aired all across the country! Fear and confusion filled my being. At first I felt exposed and tricked. After I calmed down, I realized it really didn't matter whether a few people saw me or a few million. I did my best and it would have to be okay.

It was wonderful to hear from George. In the sixties George had moved to Ontario and got a job as a welder. A few months later, George's wife, Jessie, with nine children, travelled by train across the country from Newfoundland. They'd bought a little house on Brant Street in Burlington.

In March of that year, my baby Mark, at age eleven, came in one day complaining of a sore throat. Off we went to the doctor. It was decided he would have to fly to St. Anthony Hospital to have his tonsils removed. Keith was working for Labrador Airways, so we got a free flight out. Mark was excited but a tad scared at the same time. This was all so new to him. I stayed for a few days. While I was there I went to a house party of a friend from back home. They'd seen me on the Ryan's Fancy show a few weeks earlier and knew of my dancing skills, so they wanted me to step dance for them. I was a little shy, but after a few glasses of wine I got up and did my step 'er down to my favourite tune, "St. Anne's Reel." Once that tune started playing I got itchy feet and I *had* to dance — it's in me, it's who I am … my friends said they enjoyed it.

Mark was a good patient and didn't fuss too much during the procedure. Although he remained relatively calm, I was distraught to see my baby boy in pain. But he was such a brave young man; I was proud of him. This experience brought back vivid memories of when I had my tonsils out at age twelve. Mom and I also had to fly to St. Anthony to get them out. It had been my first time in an airplane as well, and I was fascinated while crossing the Strait of Belle Isle to see such beauty and the contrast of the icebergs against the navy blue of the North Atlantic. While coming out of the anesthetic, I'd punched a nurse in the face with my fist. It was the talk of the hospital for a while.

I flew back to Goose Bay and Keith flew out to be with Mark.

In a few days Mark was well enough to return home. He and his dad flew back to Goose Bay, to the unsettling situation that lay ahead.

Keith told me of a protest that was being televised regarding Greenpeace with Brian Davies who was trying to put a stop to the annual seal hunt. It was exciting when he found out that Brigitte Bardot, the actress, was also out on the ice floes protesting the annual seal hunt. This was a big deal for Newfoundland and Labrador. The seal hunt had been going on for hundreds of years. To not allow the hunt to continue would mean hardships for the men involved. The sale of seal pelts was a financial bridge that the fishermen depended on to put them through until the start of the fishing season. Although he didn't see her in person, or close up, Keith was intrigued by being in the same town as Brigitte Bardot.

I was still working for the Canadian mess hall and trying to adjust to an eight-hour day. Then one day as the summer approached, I started thinking of George and Jessie's offer. I decided to talk to Keith about the possibility of going on that trip to Burlington, or even moving out of Goose Bay for good. Mind you, we had no savings. How could we even think of such a thing? Keith was very involved in the community. He was a golfer and spent a lot of time at the golf club during the day and he was now the newly elected president of the Squirrel Club and spent his evenings there. He was also a swimming instructor and taught adult swimming classes once a week. I was still teaching swimming and our children loved to swim as well. The parties were still happening and as a young couple in a robust community we had a lot of friends. Things were great until Keith would have too much to drink, and his jealously would override reason and the fight would be on once again.

In June, I decided it was time to have another conversation about the trip to Ontario. It sounded like a wonderful plan, but how could we swing it? Suddenly, it dawned on me — for years we'd been hearing stories of civilians getting travel warrants from the Canadian military to go on vacation. It was one of the government's ways of compensating us for living in isolated parts of the country, such as Labrador. Keith didn't qualify because he didn't work for them, but I did. Why *not* us? It was certainly worth a try.

"Who do I go see to find out?" I asked one day.

"Your boss or the officer in charge of the mess."

"I'll go next week to see what they say," I told Keith.

It sounded like we had made a decision to visit Ontario. We told no one of our plans. I approached the office of the warrant officer shaking in my shoes. I told him of my plans; I asked if it was possible to get a ticket to fly our whole family to Ontario.

"I think there just might be something still in place. I'll look into it right away, Josie," he said.

I walked out of his office with a little hope. Neither of us had ever been outside of the province.

The very next day I was called into the office. My boss had a pleasant look on his face.

"I have good news, Josie. We can get you a ticket to fly your family to Montreal, would that suffice?"

"Oh yes, sir. That would be wonderful," I said, trying to hold back my excitement.

"When do you plan to go?" he asked.

"I'm not sure yet, sir. I'll let you know as soon as I find out."

Suddenly my head was spinning. I barely knew what geography meant let alone the cost to fly to Montreal or the distance from there to Burlington. I was too proud to ask. All that mattered was that we were going. I couldn't wait to tell Keith the good news. We made plans for August, and phoned Jessie to tell them. George said he would drive to Montreal to pick us up. We had plans, big plans. If we could find work and a place to live, maybe we would not return. We decided we needed to keep it a secret.

I have no idea how the news got out that we might be leaving the Goose. Rumours flew like wild fire. "No, Keith and Josie would never leave here," and on and on and on the news spread throughout the community.

To most people this was no big deal, but for my family this was a *very* big deal. While I was making all the arrangements, Keith continued to do his thing: golf and drink with his buddies, play poker at the club, and whatever else he wanted to do. He just seemed to agree with whatever I planned, and was oblivious as to what it all entailed. What was wrong with this picture? Why could I not demand more of him? Why did I put up with his lack of help and support?

The following weeks and months were far from uneventful. I had things to do! As the summer was flying by, we attended several parties. Our friends still didn't want to believe we were leaving for good. They could accept the fact we were going on a vacation, but never to leave forever.

In the meantime, I needed to make plans. I had to find a way to ship our furniture and make arrangements with the Canadian National Railway as to how to get our goods from Goose Bay to a train station in Montreal, as there was no railway in Goose Bay. I had to talk to the school system about transferring the children, get everything packed that we'd planned to bring with us, and find buyers for the rest.

Filled with apprehension, I went into the office to fill out the government forms for the travel warrant. Would we qualify? I then had to focus on all the other things: pool keys to hand in, the children's teachers to talk to, and cars to sell. The list was endless, it seemed. I was in a daze. Was this actually happening?

I wondered what would happen if we didn't return. Would we have to repay the money for the tickets? I pushed that thought aside; we'd worry about that if and when the time came. We were elated! Keith phoned his brother and plans were in place to pick us up in Montreal.

Many questions kept popping up in my mind, but who would I ask? Who would have the answers? I was serving an officer his dinner at the mess one evening. There were several other officers in the room as well. I mustered up the courage to ask a few questions.

"Are there any high schools in Burlington?"

"Oh yes, it has eight high schools."

"Eight? How big is Burlington then?" I asked.

"It has a population of about 80,000 people," one of the other men said. He was actually from Burlington!

"Wow, that's more than the whole of Labrador," I gasped. I was stunned.

A few days later I picked up my travel warrant and, clutching it tightly in my hand, I wept. Could we actually be going to, what seemed to me, a strange world? Would we actually be able to create a new and better life for our children? Through exhausting work, determination, and grit, I'd get everything done.

We had handed in the keys to the house, and the children said tearful goodbyes to their friends. However, they were unusually quiet and didn't say much as to what was happening. Was it because they had no concept of the outside world? I may have overlooked the most important thing of all — our children. Did they even want to go away forever, to leave their lifelong friends? All I was thinking of was their future, to get them out of Goose Bay, and hopefully to have a better life.

Keith got into a ruckus at the club again. I didn't know this until a couple of days before we were to leave. It happened when he handed the club keys over to the vice president. An argument started, and Keith hit another member. A few days later, Keith bumped into Hayward Spearing in the Valley. He told Keith the Royal Canadian Mounted Police were looking for him. Apparently, the guy he'd gotten into a fight with several days earlier had pressed charges. If they found Keith before we left, we would *not* be permitted to leave. I was livid! Keith was very concerned that the cops would be out looking for him. We had to devise a plan.

The plan was to leave the children at our empty house, even though there were no beds left for them to sleep in. We didn't object, because it's what they wanted to do. People didn't worry about break-ins, kidnappings, or crime of any sort in Goose Bay at that time, but just in case, we instructed them to not answer the door and to keep it locked. Keith turned out all the lights and left them in the dark. As for the two of us, luckily our friends came to our rescue. They invited us to stay at their place in Spruce Park for the night. We were extremely grateful to them for the kind offer. We spent the night having a few drinks and reminiscing over the years we'd spent together, the good times and the bad. Tearfully, we finally went off to bed. As one can imagine, very little sleep was had by anyone. Fear, as never before, engulfed me throughout the night. I worried about the kids alone and in the dark. The only light they had filtered through from the house lights and streetlights outside. However, it was still a terrible situation to leave them in. I cried silently into my pillow as I worried about them.

The kids later told me that they never forgot their last night in Goose Bay. Greg said he'd spent the whole night in the dark because they weren't allowed to turn on the lights. Darlene said that when she got home from visiting a friend in the Valley she tripped over a pile of frying pans on the floor. Cathy said she'd slept on a dresser, while Mark bunked down wherever he could find a spot upstairs in the dark. We *had* to catch that flight in the morning — at all cost!

On August 4, we were all packed and ready to go. Finally, blissful daylight started creeping through the windows, and I became over-whelmed with gratitude. We thanked our friends for allowing us to stay with them. We said tearful goodbyes and left to collect our children. There was no one there to wish us luck, no one to say we'll miss you, no one to wish us a nice time — nothing. The kids remained strangely quiet. What were they thinking, I wondered. As we stepped outside in the cool clear August morning, there was a light frost on the ground. The sun had just hit it, making it appear like a giant silver carpet. It was a beautiful sight to behold.

We drove to the airport, terrified the Mounties would catch up with us. When we entered the plane, there were several RCMP officers on board. We practically stopped breathing. Were they waiting for Keith to board? We dared not look up as we settled into our seats. As the plane taxied into position and lifted off the ground, Keith and I gave each other a look of pure gratitude and relief. We were safe. We were off to a brand new world. We would not be returning. The Mounties got off in Wabush, they weren't chasing us after all …

We were free!

Epilogue

In chapter twenty-two I talk briefly about Keith's childhood, and through-out the book I talk of his heavy drinking and all that it entails. Keith is a self-admitted alcoholic. He drank and gambled heavily for thirty years. He quit drinking in 1988. There's a booklet out that talks about a dry drunk. They still have all the symptoms of an active alcoholic: jealously, anger, impatience, negativity, and difficulty communicating. Keith had all of those.

We were both damaged people and it took a lot of hard work to crawl out of the hole of self-pity, and all the other symptoms listed above. We get along beautifully today. Although he's a tad opinionated and likes to be in control to some degree, he has mellowed out considerably. He has become the most sensitive, gentle, and kind-hearted person one would be pleased to know.

Five years ago we talked for three whole days while driving back from Labrador. *Everything* was put on the table, and as a result we have no secrets today. We trust each other, and more importantly we love each other deeply. On June 30, 2013, we celebrated our fifty-second anniversary.

Also by Josie Penny

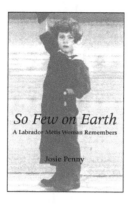

So Few on Earth
A Labrador Métis Woman Remembers
9781554887095
$26.99

Josephine Mildred Curl Penny grew up in Labrador during the 1940s and 1950s. Like many Métis, she and her family lived a semi-nomadic lifestyle, moving *inside* to the primitive settlement of Roaches Brook each fall to hunt and trap, and *outside* to Spotted Islands in the spring to harvest the rich fishing grounds.

Sent away to hospital at age four, to boarding school when she was seven, and forced out to work at age eleven, Josie lost the family bond so important to a young child. She recounts the years spent at Lockwood Boarding School where she suffered atrocious punishments, merciless teasing, and the humiliation of two rapes. The depersonalization and constant punishment eventually took their toll, and her once free-spirited nature was broken. Reading became her only escape.

Set against the beauty and ruggedness of the Labrador coast, *So Few on Earth* is a story of perseverance in a harsh environment and the possibility of life starting anew from shattered beginnings.

Of Related Interest

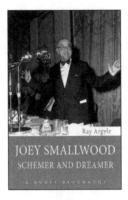

Joey Smallwood
Schemer and Dreamer
by Ray Argyle
9781459703698
$19.99

Born in Gambo, Newfoundland, Joseph ("Joey") Smallwood (1900–1991) spent his life championing the worth and potential of his native province. Although he was a successful journalist and radio personality, Smallwood is best known for his role in bringing Newfoundland into Confederation with Canada in 1949, believing that such an action would secure an average standard of living for Newfoundlanders. He was rightfully dubbed the "only living Father of Confederation" in his lifetime and was premier of the province for twenty-three years.

During much of the last part of the twentieth century, Smallwood remained a prominent player in the story of Newfoundland and Labrador's growth as a province. Later in life he put himself in debt in order to complete his *Encyclopedia of Newfoundland and Labrador*, the only project of its kind in Canada up to that point.

In *Joey Smallwood: Schemer and Dreamer*, Ray Argyle re-examines the life of this incredible figure in light of Newfoundland's progress in recent years, and measures his vision against its new position as a province of prosperity rather than poverty.

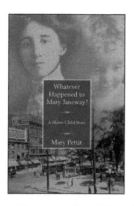

Whatever Happened to Mary Janeway?
A Home Child Story
by Mary Pettit
9781459701717
$26.99

Sixteen-year-old Mary Janeway, a home child, is desperate to escape from her rural home child placement and flees to London, Ontario, to find a domestic position. When conditions become unbearable, she moves on, vowing never to relinquish her freedom again.

After she arrives in Hamilton as a young bride, she quickly adapts to the urban conveniences and the marvels of new inventions that include electric sewing machines, sulphur matches, street stoplights, a one-horsepower Brunswick refrigerator, the advent of the zipper, and the beginning of radio. But even the latest technology can't stop the ravages of disease and other family tragedies.

Mary lives through two world wars, the Spanish Influenza, and the Great Depression. In spite of many hardships, she remains a strong, resilient woman well into her senior years and makes many contributions to Hamilton, the city she calls home.

Available at your favourite bookseller

DUNDURN

Visit us at
Dundurn.com
@dundurnpress
Facebook.com/dundurnpress
Pinterest.com/dundurnpress